Thomas Barlow

Popery

The principles and positions approved by the Church of Rome - when really believ'd and practis'd - are very dangerous to all

Thomas Barlow

Popery

The principles and positions approved by the Church of Rome - when really believ'd and practis'd - are very dangerous to all

ISBN/EAN: 9783337126407

Printed in Europe, USA, Canada, Australia, Japan

Cover: Foto ©Lupo / pixelio.de

More available books at **www.hansebooks.com**

POPERY:

OR, THE

Principles & Positions

Approved by the

CHURCH

OF

ROME

(*When Really Believ'd and Practis'd*)
Are very Dangerous to all; and to *Protestant Kings and Supreme Powers*, more especially Pernicious:

And Inconsistent with *that Loyalty*, which (by the Law of *NATURE* and *SCRIPTURE*) is Indispensably due to SUPREME POWERS.

In a LETTER to a Person of Honor;

By T. Ld Bishop of LINCOLN.

Rev. 18. 4. Jer. 15. 6.
Come out of her my people, least ye be partakers of her Sins and Plagues.

In the *SAVOY*:
Printed by *T. Newcomb*, and sold by *James Collins* in the *Temple-passage* from *Essex-street*. 1679.

FOR MY
HONORED FRIEND
L. N. P.

SIR,

Received and read your Letter, and this comes to (bring my humble Service, and) tell you so. In your Letter you tell me, *First*, Of an Inhumane and Bloody Design and Popish Plot, a Traiterous and Roman-Catholick Conspiracy (as you call it) against the Sacred Person and Life of our Gracious King (whom God preserve) and many more (by them) design'd for Ruine, and for the Subversion of the true Religion Establish'd by Law, and introducing Papal Tyranny, Superstition and Idolatry. A design not onely Unchristian, but Inhumane and Barbarous; beyond all examples of Turkish or Pagan cruelty; nor has it (in any story)

[2]   Popish Principles, &c.

(a) Nuptiæ Parisinæ & Laniena Protestantium in Gallia. Anno 1572. Vide Thuanum.

story) any parallel Impiety; unless perhaps, that Bloody (a) *French* Massacre, or the *Gun-powder-Treason*; all contriv'd and carry'd on, by Men of the same desperate Principles, and (though with the blood and ruine of many thousand innocent persons) to advance the Papal Interest. *Secondly*, You say, That the Popish Party decry this Impious Conspiracy, as a State-Trick (without truth or reallity) to make Catholicks (as they commonly miscall themselves) odious to the People, and this whole Nation. This I believe (and know) they do. As their Plots and Conspiracies, so their Impudence to deny or lessen them (when discover'd) is monstrous, and (were not their Persons and Principles known) incredible. So they did (where, and

(b) In an Almanack commonly sold, since His Majesties Happy Return; call'd *Calendarium Catholicum*; the Gun-powder-Treason is call'd, *Cecill's Contrivance*. It was printed 1661.

when they durst) and still doe (b) call the *Gun-powder-Treason*, A State-design, to make them (though they were innocent) seem guilty and Criminals. *Thirdly*. Lastly, you say, that several Papists tell you (in excuse of Popery, and their Party) That if indeed there be such a Plot and Conspiracy (as is pretended) yet it is the only fault of those persons concern'd in it, not of Popery or their Religion; the Principles and Doctrine of their Church, giving no ground or incouragement to such Impious and Anti-monarchical practices. This I believe too; because I find them making the same Apology for themselves, to take off the guilt of the Gun-powder-Treason. For (without all truth or

(c) The aforesaid Popish *Calendarium Catholicum*, or Catholick Almanack, at the end of it, about Holy-days set apart by Act of Parliament.

modesty) they tell us in Print; (c) *That the Gun-powder-Treason was* MORE THEN SUSPECTED, *to be the* CONTRIVANCE *of* Cecil, *the great Politici-*
an,

an, TO RENDER CATHOLICKS ODIOUS; *and that there were but* VERY FEW *of that Religion* (AND THOSE DESPERADOES TOO) *detected of it,* &c. *All* (d) *sober Catholicks detesting that, and all such Conspiracies.*

Now these things premis'd, you desire to know of me, whether I think these their Allegations and Apologies true; or if I think them untrue and insignificant (as you may be sure I do) that I would give you some reasons why I do so. In obedience therefore to your command, and to satisfie that Obligation that lies upon me (so far as I am able) to Vindicate Truth, and my Mother the Church of *England*; (though I have little time, and few Books here (being absent from my own) save what I borrow of friends) I shall endeavour to say something, which may (I hope) be pertinent, towards the conviction of our Adversaries, and your satisfaction. And here, I shall plainly set down,

(d) And yet *Ribedaneira, Bzovius,* &c. reckon those Gunpowder Traytors amongst the eminent *Martyrs* for their Church and Religion; as you shall see anon. And Father *Parsons* calls *Garnet* (Executed for High Treason, and the Gunpowder Conspiracy)........ *An Innocent Man, who suffer'd Unjustly; that he lived a* SAINTS *Life, and accomplish'd the same with an* HAPPY DEATH, *dying in* DEFENCE *of* JUSTICE. In his Book against the Oath of Allegiance; call'd, *Discussion of the Answer of Dr. William Barlow,* &c. p. 22, 23.

I The *Position* I undertake to make good.
II. The *Proofs* and Reasons of it.

I. The *Position* is this.....*The Doctrine and Principles of Popery, own'd by the Church of* Rome *(when believed and practised) are not onely dangerous, but pernicious to Kings (especially those who are Protestants) prejudicial to the just rights of Monarchy, and inconsistent with that Loyalty, which (by the Laws of Nature and Scripture) is due to them; and particularly to our Kings, by the establish'd and known Laws of* England, *made antiently, even by Popish*

B 2 *Kings*

Kings and *Parliaments*, *against Papal Usurpations, and Anti-monarchical practices*. And here (becaufe it is impoffible diftinctly to fhew, how Popifh Principles are dangerous to our Kings, and prejudicial to their Juft Rights, and Royal Prerogative; unlefs we firft know, what that Prerogative, and thofe Rights are) I fhall inquire,

1. What the *Jura Coronæ*, the Rights and Prerogatives of the Imperial Crown of *England* are, as to our prefent concern.
2. How Popifh Doctrines and Principles, may be dangerous, or pernicious to them.

1. For the *Firft*; That *England* is a Monarchy, the *Crown Imperial*, and our Kings *SUPREME* Governors, and *SOLE SUPREME Governors* of this Realm, and all other their Dominions, will (I believe, I am fure it fhould) be granted; feeing our Authentick Laws and Statutes do fo exprefly, and fo often fay it. In our Oath of Supremacy we Swear, that the King is, the *ONELY SUPREME Governor*. *SUPREME*, fo none (not the Pope) above Him: and *ONELY Supreme*: fo none coordinate, or equal to Him. So that by our known Laws, our King is, *Solo Deo minor*, invefted with *fuch a Supremacy*, as excludes both Pope and People. (and all the World, God Allmighty onely excepted, by whom Kings Reign) from having any power, jurifdiction, or authority over Him. For this

Soveraignty

Soveraignty and *Supremacy* belonging to our Kings, and the Imperial Crown of *England* is afferted, not onely by the Statutes of (*e*) Q. *Elizabeth*, (*f*) King *James*, and (*g*) *Charles* the Second (Proteftant Princes) but even thofe Statutes made by Popifh Princes and Parliaments, declare the fame: I Inftance onely in (*h*) *Richard* the Second, (*i*) *Henry* the Eighth, and (*k*) Q. *Mary* (though all the Statutes of Provifors, were pertinent to this purpofe.) That *Richard* the Second and His Parliament were Roman-Catholicks, is manifeft; and it is as certain, that *Henry* the Eighth and His Parliaments (when the Statutes cited were made) were fo too. For 'tis evident, that thofe Statutes were made *Anno* 24. and *Anno* 25. *Hen*. 8. that is, *Anno Dom*. 1532. and 1533. when neither He, nor His Adherents, were Excommunicate, but actual Members of the Roman Church then, and for fome years after. For though Pope *Paul* the Third was angry, and about it, *Anno* 1535. yet he did not actually Excommunicate Him or His Adherents, before the year (*l*) 1538. which was fix years after *Henry* the Eighth, and His Popifh Parliament had Vindicated the Rights of the Imperial Crown of *England*, againft the irrational and unjuft Pretences and Ufurpations of the Pope; and declared, that the *Supremacy* (both in Ecclefiaftical and Civil Things) ever did (*de Jure*) belong to the Imperial Crown of *England*, not to the Pope's Mitre: He having no more to do in *England*, (*Jure proprio*, or by any Law of God or Man) than *Henry* the Eighth in *Italy*. And that Parliament of Queen *Mary*, (cited in the Margent) although a Popifh Parliament,

(*e*) Vid. Statut. 1 Eliz. cap. 1. 5 Eliz. cap. 1. & 13 Eliz. cap. 2.
(*f*) Vid. 1 Jac. cap. 7. & 3 Jac. cap. 4.
(*g*) Vid. 12 Car. 2. cap. 30. In the Preamble.
(*h*) Statut. 16 Rich. 2. cap. 5.
(*i*) Statut. 24 Hen. 8. cap. 12. & 25 Hen. 8. cap. 19. & 37 Hen. 8. cap. 17. & 25 Hen. 8. cap. 1.
(*k*) Parliamentum fecundum 2 Mariæ, cap. 1.

(*l*) The *Bull* by which *Hen*. 8. was Excommunicate, was Dat. Romæ 16. Cal. Januarii, Pauli Papæ 3. Anno 5. Vid. Bullarium Cherutini, Tom. 1. pag. 704. Edit. Lugduni, 1655.

Parliament, yet declares fully for the Queen's Supremacy (which to some may seem strange) for that Act expresly says, 1. *That the IMPERIAL CROWN of this Realm, with all its Prerogatives, Jurisdictions,* &c. *was descended to the Queen.* 2. That she was the *SOVERAIGN and SUPREME Governour* of all Her Dominions, in *AS FULL, LARGE, and AMPLE MANNER, AS ANY OF HER PROGENITORS,* (therefore in as ample a manner as Her Father *Henry* the Eighth.) 3. That *by the MOST ANCIENT LAWS of this Realm, the punishment of ALL OFFENDERS, against the Regality and Laws of this Realm, belong'd to the King, &c.* So that even a Popish Parliament acknowledges and declares, the Kings of *England* possess'd of such a Supremacy, over all Persons, and that by our MOST ANCIENT LAWS, that He may punish ALL OFFENDERS (Clergy or Laity) against the Laws, and His Regality. (How contradictory to this, the *Trent* Council and the Doctrine of the Roman Church is, you shall see anon.) But for the Supremacy of the Kings of *England,* according to our *Ancient and Later Laws*, I refer you to the (*m*) Learned in those Laws; who will give you a clear Declaration of this Supremacy, and a just Vindication of it, from those impertinent (and seditious) Objections brought against it by some, who, inslaved to *Rome*, have cast off Loyalty to their King, and Love to their Country.

And lastly, As for the Supremacy of Kings, (so far as it concerns the Laws of God, (Natural or Positive) and Divines to determine it) I refer you to

(*m*) Vid. *Coke's* Reports, Part 5. de Jure Regis Ecclesiastico; and *Calvin's* Case, 7 Report; Sir *John Davis* his Reports, in the Case of *Præmunire*, &c.

to the *Answer of the* (n) *University of Oxon*, to a
Letter of *Henry* the Eighth, requiring their Judgment in that Point: To the (o) *Articles of Edward the Sixth*; Of Queen (p) *Elizabeth*; The *Articles* (q) of *Ireland*; The (r) *Injunctions of Elizabeth*; The (s) *Canons* of 1. *Jacobi*; And the (t) *Canons* (*sub Carolo Martyre*) 1640. (besides the Writings of many particular Learned Men:) In which you may see the Judgment of the Church of *England*, concerning Supremacy, and the *Loyalty due to our King*, clearly and fully express'd; and (in the late unhappy Rebellion) more truly profess'd and practic'd by Her Sons, than Papist, Presbyter, or Fanatique (though some of them vainly brag of their Loyalty) can, with any just reason pretend to. If you desire further satisfaction and evidence, for the *Supremacy of Kings*, (particularly of our Kings, and the *Roman Emperours*) even in *Ecclesiastical Matters*, you know, and (at your leisure) may consult, the Collections of our (u) *Saxon*, and the (w) *Imperial* Laws; where you may have sufficient and abundant evidence, that (as to Matter of Fact; never questioned in those days) those Emperours and Kings, made many Laws and Constitutions, in Ecclesiastical Matters, (which concerned the Church) as well as Civil, (which concern'd the State.) And (if you desire it) I can shew you, an Original MS. (*agreed upon*, and *approved* by the Convocations of both Provinces, (*Canterbury* and *York*) and subscribed by both Archbishops, and several of each Province) wherein it is clearly shewn, (so far as Scripture, and other Records of those times mention

(n) Vid. Literas Acad. Oxon. Hen. 8. Dat. 17 Jul. 1534.

(o) Art. Ed. 6. 1552. Art. 36.

(p) Art. 5 Eliz. 1562. Art. 37.

(q) Articuli Hiberniæ, 1615. Sect. 57.

(r) Editæ 1559. in calce post Injunctionem, 53.

(s) Canones 1603. Can. 1, 2.

(t) Can. 1640. Can. 1. &c.

(u) See our Saxon Laws by Mr. *Lambert*, *Spelman* Concil. Tom. 7. Whelogus, &c.

(w) Vid. Cod. Theodosianum, cum Doctiss. Gothofred. Notis, & Cod. & Novellas Constitut. Justiniani.

tion them) that Kings (from the beginning of the World, till our Blessed Saviours time) did, and *de Jure*, might exercise an Ecclesiastical, as well as Civil Jurisdiction and Supremacy; especially the Kings of the Jews, his own People; which Monarchy was of Gods own, (and particularly Divine) Institution. These things premis'd, I come now to shew you, (in the second place) how dangerous, and (when, and where they have power to put them in execution) how pernicious Popish Principles are, to the Persons of Kings, and their just Rights and Prerogatives. And here, I say,

1. That many of their *Popish Principles*, and generally approved and *received Doctrines*, are not only dangerous, but destructive to, and inconsistent with the just Soveraignty and Supremacy of Kings. Because they generally say, and (in a thousand Books Writ to that purpose) industriously endeavour to prove it, That all Kings and Emperours, are so far from being Supreme, that they are Subject to the Pope, as to their Superiour Lord, to whom they owe Service and Fidelity. That this may appear, consider,

(x) *Cæsar, ut primum Pontificem videt, illum DETECTO CAPITE, genu TERRAM TANGENS, VENERATUR; & iterum, cum appropinquet ad gradus sedis Papæ, genuflectit; ac demum, cum ad Pontificis pedes pervenerit, illos DEVOTE osculatur. Sacrarum Ceremon. Sanctæ Rom. Ecclesiæ, Lib.* 1. Tit. 5. Pag. 22. Col. 3. Editionis Rom. Anno 1560.

1. The Emperour, (x) *when he comes into the Popes presence, as soon as ever he sees him, he must (His Hat off, and bare-headed) bow, till his Knee touch the ground, and worship the Pope; and coming nearer, must bow again; and when he comes to the Pope, he must bow a third time, and* DEVOUTLY *Kiss the Popes Foot.* The Emperour must WORSHIP the Pope, with the Incurvations, or bowings of Body, even to the ground, and then (bareheaded,

headed, and on his Knees) DEVOUTLY Kiss the Pope's Foot. Execrable and prodigious Pride! The Pope (without all truth or probability) vainly and ridiculously, only pretends to be Christ's Vicar, and so (if it were true) is less than his Master; and yet our blessed Saviour never requir'd, nor had such Adorations, Incurvations, or Kissings of his Toe, of any, much less of Kings or Emperors. Nor would any Man require such, but the (y) *Man of Sin*; who *exalts himself* (takes that greatness which God never gave him) *above all that is call'd God, or worshiped:* That is, above all. *Kings* and *Emperors.* Well, but does not the Pope (in this Case) shew some respect and civility to the Emperor? Does he not uncover his head, or bow his body, &c. Noe; for the same Authentick Book, of the *SACRED Ceremonies*, of the *HOLY Roman* Church, tells us (z)..... *That the Pope never gives any reverence, to ANY MORTAL whomsoever, either by rising up apparently, or by uncovering, or bowing his head. Onely* (sayes that Ceremonial) *when the Emperor has kiss'd the Foot of the Pope, sitting in his Chair, he riseth up, A VERY LITTLE to him; and so he does sometimes to GREAT PRINCES.* Whether this can stand with that Supremacy, which (by Divine Law, Natural and Positive) is due to Kings, to be so far subject, and slaves to the Pope; let Kings (who are most concern'd) and the World Judge. And it is to be considered, that the Book I cite for those passages concerning the Pope, is no *Apocryphal*, or *Non-licenc'd Pamphlet*, containing the inventions of some private person; but it contains the *SACRED Ceremonies* of

(y) 2 Thess. 2. vers. 3 4.

(z) *Pontifex Romanus NEMINI omnino mortalium reverentiam facit, assurgendo manifeste, caput inclinando, aut detegendo. Romano autem Imperatori, postquam illum SEDENS ad osculum pedis subegit, ALIQUANTULUM assurgit. Magnis etiam Principibus, PRIUSTIM adventantibus, cum NON EST in PONTIFICALIBUS, aliquantulum assurgit TANQUAM reverentiam faciens, &c.* dictus Liber Sacrar. Ceremon. Lib.3. Tit.1. Pag.113. Col. 2.

the

the ROMAN CHURCH, collected by *Marcellus* ARCHBISHOP of *Corcyra*, dedicated to POPE LEO the Tenth, printed at ROME, and highly *approved*, and (*a*) *commended* by their *eminent Writers.*

2. But this is not all; the poor Emperor muſt do (the Pope) his great Superior and Maſter, more ſervice, and be his Groome, or (at beſt) *Gentleman* (*b*) *of his Horſe.* He muſt hold the *Popes Stirrup* till he get on Horſeback, and then lead the Horſe for ſome paces (*c*) ......*Cæſar (traditis ſceptro & pomo, uni ex ſuis) prævenit ad equum Pontificis, & TENET STAPHAM, quoad Pontifex equum aſcenderit; & deinde accepto equi fræno, per aliquot paſſus ducit equum Pontificis:* and the Emperors have (*de facto*) executed this mean Office (which was impious and prodigious pride in the Pope, requiring or permitting; and degenerous in the Emperors, in performing it:) So the Emperor (*d*) *Sigiſmund* held the Stirrup of Pope *Martin* the Fifth. And the Emperor (*e*) *Frederick*, of *Alexander* the Third, &c. And the ſame *Frederick* had done the ſame to Pope *Adrian* the Fourth (if (*f*) *Baronius* ſay true) ....*In conſpectu exercitus ſui, Fridericus OFFICIUM STRATORIS cum JUCUNDITATE implevit, & ſtreguam FORTITER tenuit.* And, that it might be remember'd, *Baronius* has put this Note in the (*g*) Margent.......*Ut Reges & Imperatores INSERVIANT PAPÆ.* And in the Margent of the next Paragraph ......*Rex implet* (*h*) *munus STRATORIS Papæ.*

3. Nor is this all; the Emperor muſt Swear Fealty to the Pope; and that he will be his Proctor, to defend and maintain all his Rights and Honors, &c.

(*a*) *Liber VALDE PROBATUS*, ſayes *Poſſevin*: In Apparatu ſacro; in Chriſt. Marcello.

(*b*) He muſt execute *Stratoris Officium* (be Yeoman of the Stirrup) ſayes Card. *Baronius*. Annal. Tom. 12. ad Ann. 1177. Sect. 38.

(*c*) Dicto Sacrarum Ceremoniarum, lib. 1. Tit. 5. p. 26. Col. 3.

(*d*) *Tho. Walſingham*, Hypodig. Neuſtriæ, p. 588.

(*e*) *Baronius* Annal. Tom. 12. ad Annum. 1177. Sect. 124.

(*f*) Idem Annal. Tom. 12. ad Annum. 1155. num. 13, 14.

(*g*) *Ibid.* num. 13.

(*h*) *Ibid.* num. 14.

&c. In this form *(i)* ....*Ego Rex Romanorum futurus Imperator, promitto & juro, me de cætero Protectorem & Procuratorem fore summi Pontificis, in omnibus Necessitatibus & utilitatibus suis, custodiendo & conservando possessiones, honores, Jura,* &c. Thus Pope *Innocent* the Third made our King *John* Swear Fidelity and Allegiance to him, in this forme *(k) Ego Johannes Rex Angliæ.......fidelis ero .....Ecclesiæ Romanæ ac DOMINO MEO, Innocentio Papæ* 3, &c. And before this, Pope *Gregory* the Seventh (that Prodigy of wickedness and Papal Tyranny (sends *Hubertus* to *William* the Conqueror,*(l)* requiring him to Swear *Allegiance* and *Fidelity* to him and his Successors. 'Tis true, that the Conqueror had understanding enough to know His Royal Rights, and the Popes injust pretences, and so (as well became a King) peremptorily refused to take any such Oath. *Fidelitatem facere nolui* (sayes he in his Letters to the Pope) *nec volo*. However, *hoc Ithacus vellet*; this power they pretended to, and (as they had ability and opportunity) required it, and (we may be sure) when they have an advantage and power, they will both require, and severely (by Interdicts. Anathema's and Excommunications) exact it. And well they might, if they had that vast Power and Jurisdiction over Kings, which the Canonists, Jesuits, Schoolmen, Casuists, Summists, and their greatest Writers generally give them. I shall (of many) give you some few Instances.

4. Cardinal *Pool, (m)* after he had said, and (as he thought) proved ; That the King was the *product of the Pope and People*; by them *created* and *made King* ; and

(i) Sacrar. Ceremoniaru r S. Rom. Ecclesix. lib. 1. Tit. p. 23.

(k) Hen. de Knighton, de Eventibus Angliæ lib 2. p. 242 & Math. Westmonast. ad Annum 1213. p. 272.

(l) Ut sibi & successorib FIDELITATEM faceret. Baronius Annal. Tom 11. ad Annum 1075. num. 25.

(m) Libro ad Hen. 8. *pro Ecclesiastica Unionis Defensione.* Romæ, apud Antonium Badum Asulanum, p. 25, 26. It is in Folio, but the year when 'twas Printed not express'd.

and that the *Office of the Pope and Priest*, was the Office *of a Father*, the King being his Son. He adds ......That *Officium Patris est PRORSUS MAJUS REGIO ET DIVINIUS*. And then he has put these words (that they might be taken into special confideration) (*n*) ......*The Priest COMMANDS THE KING, but the KING CANNOT COMMAND THE PRIEST*. The *Priest* then is *superior*, and the *King* his *subject* : and so good night to the Kings Supremacy. And a little before, he sayes (*o*) ......*Henry the Eighth imitated the PRIDE of LUCIFER, when he made himself VICAR of Christ*. This is pretty well; but as the Pope desires, so the Cardinal (and others generally) give him more (*p*)......*Petri Cathedram SUPER OMNIA IMPERATORUM solia, & OMNIA REGUM tribunalia CONSTITUIT CHRISTUS*. The Pope(by their Divinity)is *Jure divino*, superior to all Kings and Emperors : And yet St. *Paul* (*q*) (*equal to St. Peter*, and far above any of his successors) acknowledges that the Emperor (*r*) and he a Pagan) was his *Judge*, and *legal superior*, and (as such) Appeals to him. *Azorius* (a great and learned perfon) confirms the Cardinals Opinion ; and tells us (*s*) *That the Emperor, BY THE LAW OF GOD, is SUBJECT to the POPE, even IN TEMPORALS.* And since him, a learned Man, and Prior General of his Order, tells us (*t*) *That the Popes EMPIRE is over ALL THE WORLD* (Pagan and Christian) *and that HE is the ONELY VICAR OF GOD, who has SUPREME power and EMPIRE, over ALL KINGS and PRINCES OF THE EARTH.* And again (*u*) ......*Sicut unus est Deus, monarcha*

(*n*) *SACERDOS in suo munere REGI PRÆCIPIT, NON CONTRA.* Ibidem. p. 65. col. 1.

(*o*) *Henricus Rex LUCIFERI SUPERBIAM imitatur, cum se ipse VICARIUM CHRISTI constituit.* Ibid. p. 7. col. 1.

(*p*) Polus Card. de Concilio, 91. Editionis in fo.

(*q*) 2. Cor. 11, 5, & 2. Cor. 12, 11.
(*r*) Act. 25, 10, 11.

(*s*) *Imperator PAPÆ JURE DIVINO SUBJECTUS, etiam in TEMPORALIBUS*, Azorius Institut. Moral. Tom. 2. lib. 10. cap. 6. p. 1041.

(*t*) *Unicus DEI VICARIUS PONTIFEX ROMANUS, habet SUMMAM potestatem & IMPERIUM super OMNES REGES & Principes TERRÆ.* Jasius Ragneus de S. Romanæ Ecclesiæ Dignitaribus. Tract. 7. p. 83.

(*u*) Ibid. p. 84.

monarcha omnium; sic inter homines, UNUS DEBET esse PRINCEPS & MONARCHA, qui OMNIBUS MORTALIBUS præsit & DOMINETUR, DEI scilicet VICARIUS. Non igitur Petrus SUB REGE, sed REGES SUB PETRO esse DEBENT, sibique & suis SUCCESSORIBUS INCURVARI TENENTUR; & COLLA SUBMITTERE. And a little after (x)........*Unus Dei Vicarius OMNIUM PRINCEPS & DOMINUS, Cui IMPERATORES REGES, & Potestates OMNES HUMILITER OBEDIANT, sintque SUBJECTI.* And good reason they should be so (if he say true) for Princes have all their power, and Authority from the Pope ......*Sicut luna accipit lumen a sole, sic REGIA potestas recepit authoritatem, NON ALIUNDE nisi A PAPA.* And for the proof of this, he cites two great (y) Lawyers (and might have cited an hundred more) *Johannes Andreas*, and *Hostiensis....*(†)*Multas rationes afferunt. Johannes Andreas & Hostiensis quibus probant, Papam esse Principem & MONARCHAM, & SUPERIOREM Laicorum omnium & & Clericorum.* Nay, 'tis THE DUTY OF ALL KINGS, to suffer the Pope to domineer over them (z)......*DEBET Potestas Spiritualis Temporali DOMINARI.* Nay, they are damn'd if they do not submit: for so the Lemma, or Title to that impious Extravagant of Pope *Boniface* the Eigth. *Omnes Christi fideles* (the Text and Glofs exprefly say it) *DE NECESSITATE SALUTIS SUBSUNT ROMANO PONTIFICI. Qui utrumque* (a) *gladium habet, & OMNES Judicat, & A NEMINE judicatur.* The Pope has both Swords that is (as their Infallible

(x) Ibid. p. 85.

(y) Ibid. p. 85.
(†) Ad Can. Nemo. 1;. & Can. Aliorum. 14. Caus. 9. Quæst. 3.

(z) Glossa ad cap. *Unam Sanctam De Majore & Obed.* in Extravag. Commun. Verbo, *ferro Jubesse*, in Resp. ad 3. Argumentum.

(a) Luc. 22. 38. 1. It cannot appear that *Peter* had them both. 2. Nor that they were given him by *Christ*. 3. Nor that they signify'd two distinct powers. 4. Nor that *Peter* might use them both, who was severely condemn'd for using one. *Matth.* 16. 51, 52.

lible Judge, the Pope, falsely and ridiculously expounds it) both the Spiritual and Temporal Power; *and is SUPREME MONARCH, above all Kings.* Nay further, they blasphemously say, that our Blessed Saviour had not done *DISCRETELY*, unless he had left such a Supreme Monarch over his Church at his Ascension, to govern the World (*b*) *.......Non videretur Dominus fuisse DISCRETUS, nisi unicum post se talem Vicarium reliquisset.*

And (to fill up the measure of their Blasphemy against God, and their sordid and impious flattery of the Pope.) Hence it is, that they declare the Pope to be *more than Man,*

(*c*) *Papa stupor mundi......Qui maxima rerum Nec Deus, nec homo, quasi neuter es inter utrumque.*

So the Gloss upon the *Clementines,* in their *Canon-Law.* And the famous Inscription (if I forget not) on an Altar at *Rome,* is as blasphemous (or rather more) as the former. The words these ; *Paulo* 5° *VICE-DEO, Pontificiæ OMNIPOTENTIÆ vindici acerrimo,* &c. where, although *VICE-DEUS,* signifie something less than God; yet *Omnipotence* blasphemously attributed to the Pope, must signifie, that he was more than Man. But there is another Gloss, which does not mince the matter, but in plain words, speaks down-right blasphemy: in which it is (*d*) *Dominus DEUS noster Papa.* So that these Glosses, though they agree in Impiety, and are both blasphemous; yet they contradict each other; the one saying, that the *Pope is God;* the other, that he is *neither*

(*b*) Glossa ad dictum Cap. *Unam Sanctam.*

(*c*) Glossa verbo Papa ad Proœmium Clementinarum.

(*d*) Glossa ad Cap. *Cum inter.* 4. verbo, *declaramus,* De Verb. Signif. in Extravag. Johan. 22.

ther *God* nor *Man*. Now, if this be true, I defire fome of their Canonifts would inform me, what they think the Pope is. For if (according to their Law) he *neither be God nor Man*; feeing (I fuppofe) it will be granted, that he is a rational Creature, and no good Angel, he muft be (by their Law and Logick) *an incarnate Devil*. I do not call him fo; but only fhew, what (by the juft confequences of their impious and blafphemous Gloffes) he muft be.

5. And here, it may not be unworthy of our obfervation, that although *Thomas Manrique* (Mafter of the facred *Palace*) in the year 1572. *thought* (e) *fit* to have this impious Glofs left out, and has (in Print) publifh'd his opinion: yet Pope (f) *Gregory* the XIII. thought otherwife, and approves and paffes this blafphemous Glofs (with fuch others) and fo it ftill remains in the (g) *Roman* and (h) *Parifian* Editions. Now although the *Congregatio Indicis*, and their Inquifitors, in their *Indices Expurgatorii*, take particular notice of, and Damn fuch Sentences as thefe (though Principles of Chriftian Religion evidently contain'd in Scripture) (i) *Abraham fide juftus* (k) *Chriftus credentibus falus*. (l) *Juftitia noftra Chriftus*. *Omnes* (m) *fumus peccatores*. I fay, though they conftantly Damn fuch Sacred Truths, and command them to be expung'd; yet this impious Glofs (making, as they think, for the Popes abfolute Monarchy) ftands untouch'd, in their laft and beft Editions of their *Canon-Law*. Onely they have in the laft Edition (I have yet feen) added this Note in the Margent, over againft the Glofs (n)..... *Hæc verba fanè*

(e) Cenfura in Gloffas Juris Canonici. Colon. 1572. p. 13, 14. & 52.

(f) Vide Bullam. ejus datam Romæ 1. Jul. 1580. præfixam Juri Canon. *Parif.* 1612.

(g) Anno 1580.
(h) Parif. 1612.

(i) Index Expurgat. Hifpan; Juxta Exemplar. Madriti 1667. pag. 99.
(k) Ibidem, p. 112. Col. 1
(l.m) Ibidem.

(n) Edit. Jur. Canon. Parif. 1612. Clement. Col. 4. in margine, ad Proæmium Clementinarum.

sano modo sunt accipienda. And that is (according to the meaning of *Johannes Andreas,* the Author of that Gloss) those words must be taken so, as they make most for the Popes Supremacy : for so it immediately follows......*Prolata enim sunt ad ostendendam amplissimam esse Pontificis Romani potestatem.*

Now this Supremacy of the Pope being granted, (which their Lawyers, Authentick Laws, their Canonists and Councils, and all their greatest Writers, *Jesuits* especially, generally contend for) it evidently follows, that the Pope is the sole and onely Supreme Power on Earth; and so all Kings and Emperors are, and must be his subjects, and so must lose that Supremacy, which (by the Laws of Nature and Scripture) does *de Jure* belong to them. For they say, and industriously endeavor to prove this Absolute Supreme Power and Monarchy of the Pope, over all Kings and Emperors in the World. I shall, to satisfie you, bring two or three more Witnesses to prove it.

I. *Abraham* (o) *Bzovius* tells us, 1. That the *Pope is MONARCH of ALL CHRISTIANS* (Kings and Emperors included.) 2. That he is *SUPREME over ALL MORTALS.* 3. That there lies no *APPEALE from him.* 4. That he is *JUDGE of HEAVEN,* and in all *EARTHLY JUDGMENTS SUPREME.* 5. That he is, *THE ARBITRATOR of THE WORLD.* These (and many more such) *Bzovius* industriously indeavors to prove out of all their Popish Authors. Nor is his Book any surreptitious work, clandestinely publish'd, such

---

(o) Abrah. Bzovius de Pontifice Romano. Coloniæ Agrip. 1619. sayes,
1. *Papa est Christianorum Monarcha,* cap. 1.
2. *Mortalium supremus,* cap. 3.
3. *A quo Provocatio nulla,* cap. 16.
4. *Judex cœli, & in Judicio terreno supremus,* cap. 12.
5. *Arbiter Orbis,* cap. 45.

such as *Rome* would not own; for it comes out, with all the Solemn Approbations and Commendations of his Superiors, and the *Apostolick Inquisitor*; who thus approves *Bzovius* his Book (and so all the above-mention'd Extravagant and Antimonarchical Positions) (p) ..... *Seeing it sufficiently appears, by the AP-PROBATIONS of the DOCTORS, and the Authors FAMOUS NAME; that the Learning of this present Work is SINGULAR, and the DOCTRINE SOLID, both IN FAITH and MANNERS; therefore I think it fit to be publish'd, FOR THE COMMON UTILITY.* So that this Doctrine of the Popes Supremacy, above all Kings and Emperors, is not *Bzovius* his private Opinion, but has the Approbation of the Roman Church (at least in the Judgment of those who approved it) being attested by those, who (by that Church) are impowered for that purpose.

II. My next Witness is *Isiodorus Mosconius.* (Vicar-General to the Archbishop of *Bononia*, and a learned Lawyer) who tells us (*q*)......*That the Pope is UNIVERSAL JUDGE, KING OF KINGS, and LORD of LORDS, because his power is of God; That GODS TRIBUNAL and the POPES, is one and the SAME, and that they have the SAME CONSISTORY: and therefore ALL other powers are HIS SUBJECTS, and that the Pope is JUDGED of NONE BUT GOD, not of THE EMPEROR or KINGS, or of the CLERGY or LAITY.*

(p) Vide Approbationes libro Brovii, De Pontifice Romano præfixas; in Approbatione Inquisitoris Apostolici....... *Cum de presentis Operis SINGULARI eruditione, SOLIDAQUE IN FIDE AC MORIBUS DOCTRINA, tam ex DOCTORUM CALCULO, quam ex Authoris CELEBRI NOMINE, satis CONSTET, censeo ut ad COMMUNEM UTILITATEM excudatur, &c.*

(q) Isiod. Mosconius, de Majest. Ecclesiæ Militantis. lib. 1. cap. 7. p. 26. Venetiis 1602. *Pontifex Rom. est Judex universalis, Rex Regum, & Dominus Dominantium, eo quod ejus potestas a Deo est, & nullum habet superiorem nisi Deum: estque unum Tribunal inter Deum & Papam. Ideo omnes aliæ potestates ei subditæ sunt, & a nemine judicatur, nisi a Deo; non ab Augusto, non a Regibus, nec a Clero aut populo.* Et p. 640. in Margine, *Papa est omnium Principum Monarcha,* &c.

And

And he cites many of their Canons and Councils, which (as positively as he) say and prove the same thing.

III. *Celsus Mancinus* (De Juribus Principatuum Romæ 1596. lib. 3. cap 1. 2.) is not far short, in attributing an *absolute supreme power to the Pope,* even in Temporal things. For (in the place cited) he tells us *Three* things (which he fully proves, out of their best Authors.) (r) 1. That the Pope *is* LORD OF THE WHOLE WORLD. 2. That the Pope (as Pope) has TEMPORAL POWER. 3. That this temporal power of the Pope, is, of ALL OTHER POWERS in the World MOST EMINENT; *and* ALL other Powers DEPEND *on the* POPE. But let this pass; I shall cite you a greater Authority which will not onely tell you, that the Papal Power is greater then Regal and Imperial, but how much it is greater, for

IV. Pope Innocent the III. (as *Infallible* as any of his Successors) tells us, that the Papal (ſ) Power, is as much greater than the Imperial, as *the* SUN *is greater than the* MOON. And the Gloss there (t) sayes, that is 47 *times* greater. He who put the Note in the Margent there, thinks this too little; and therefore he sayes, *Quinquagies septies*; The Papal Power is (according to his Arithmetick) 57 times greater than the Imperial. A man would think, that (by these accounts) the Popes Power were great enough. But there is

---

(r) Mancinus loco citato, ait. 1. *Papa est* TOTIUS ORBIS DOMINUS. 2. *PAPA* (*ut Papa*) *habet* POTESTATEM TEMPORALEM. 3. *Potestas Papæ temporalis, est* OMNIUM *aliarum Potestatum* EMINENTISSIMA, *aliæque potestates* OMNES *ab illo* DEPENDENT.

(ſ) Innocentius 3. cap. *Solicitæ*, 6. Extra de *Major. & Obedientiæ.*

(t) *Pontificalis dignitas quadragies septies Regali major.* to the learned Cleſs.

is an Addition there (who was the Author of
it, I know not) in which we are told (you
may believe so far as you think fit) that the
Papal Dignity exceeds the Imperial, no less than
7744. so inconsiderable a thing (in these mens
account) is Regal and Imperial Majesty, in respect of the Vast greatness of Papal Supremacy.

In short; if you compare that Decretal of *Innocent* the Third (but now cited) with that famous
Extravagant of Pope (*u*) *Boniface* the Eighth (both
which are received into the body of their Canon-Law) you will find them cite several places of
Scripture (miserably misunderstood) and bring reasons to prove the Papal Power above the Regal and
Imperial. But the consequences they draw from
those Texts they cite, are so far from being Infallible, that they are (like those who cite them)
evidently false; and what other Arguments they
bring, are not onely unlike-reason, but ridiculous:
yet although neither the Reasons, nor the Authority of their Popes, nor the general consent of the
ablest Writers *Rome* has (who all endeavour to
establish the same Position, and the Popes extravagant Supremacy) can prove that he really has such
power (nor are they cited by me to any such purpose) yet they clearly prove that they own that
doctrine (which is all I aim at) and (though they
cannot) gladly would make it appear probable, and
have us and all others to believe it.

6. And further, from this unlimited Supremacy
of the Pope, they conclude (and publickly profess)
his

(*u*) Bonifacius. 8. cap. U-
nam Sanctam. 1. De majoritate & Obed. Extrav. Com.

his *power to depose Kings*, absolve their Subjects from all Oathes of Allegiance, and dispose of their Kingdoms. That this may appear, I consider,

1. That to cite particular Popish Writers, would be endless, and needless; that *Bellarmine, Emanuel Sa, Suares, Mariana, Turrecremata*, &c. that the Canonists, Casuists, Schoolmen, Summists, Jesuits, &c. are generally (if not universally) of this opinion, (*That the Pope may depose Kings*, &c.) is notoriously known to all, who know them. I shall onely instance in two or three (to give you a taste of that impious doctrine, which all of them profess, assert, and (so far as they are able) vindicate, &c.) And here, 1. *Celsus Mancinus* (a learned Canon-Regular of the Order of St. *Augustine*) tells us, that (x)... *It is* EVIDENT TO ALL, THAT EMPERORS ARE DEPOSED and DEPRIVED *by the Pope*, *and that not* ONELY FOR *things pertaining* TO FAITH, *but* ALSO *for things pertaining to* MANNERS *and the* CIVIL LAW. And *Abraham Bzovius* (more fully) sayes, (as generally the rest doe.) 1. (y) *That the secular power* IS SUBJECT *to the* SPIRITUAL ; *so that it is no usurpation*, *if the Spiritual* JUDGE *the Secular*. 2. *The Pope has* SUPREME POWER *over Christian* KINGS *and* PRINCES, *who may* CORRECT, DEPOSE, *and* PUT OTHERS *in their* PLACES. 3 *The Pope may* DEPRIVE *a* KING *of his Royal Dignity for* HERESY, SCHISME, *for any intollerable crime, negligence, or laziness* , *if in great matters he break his Oath, or oppress the Church,* &c. So that *in all these cases* (by him there mention'd, and they

are

are Eight or Nine) *the Pope may depose a Supreme Prince*; and the Pope himself is SOLE JUDGE both of the CRIME and Condemnation. And to make all this good, 1. He gives us a (*z*) Catalogue of above Thirty Kings and Princes, who have *(de facto)* been Deposed, or (by Excommunications and Anathema's) Damn'd by the Pope. 2. And then he cites the Canon of a (*) General Council of their own, (of which anon) and above an hundred eminent Authors of their own Church, who assert and justifie that Impious Opinion. 3. And then he further adds, that AN INNUMERABLE company of ENGLISH MARTYRS (following their Captain *Edmund Campian*, a *Villain* Condemned and Executed for (†) *High Treason)* did with their Pens and Blood maintain the same Opinion.—*IN-NUMERABILES etiam Anglicani MARTYRES DU-CEM Edmundum CAMPIANUM secuti, pro PRI-MATU Romani Pontificis, ab Hen. 8. & Elizabethæ cæsi, Sanguine profuso, & stilo exerto, idem docuerunt.* So that we may see, the Doctrine of the Pope's Power to DEPOSE KINGS, must be *de fide*, an Article of Divine Truth, and They Martyrs who Die in Defence of it : for *Campian* is with them, a (*) *Most FAMOUS MARTYR*.

These Positions, asserted publickly and in Print, by Popish Authors, with so much confidence, and without any check of the Romish Church, of which they are Members ; may justly seem impious and horrid to any sober Christian, who wishes well (as all good Subjects should) to Kings and Monarchy : yet I shall shew you greater Abominations. One
of

(*z*) Bzovius loco citato, pag. 611. 612, &c.

(*) Ibid. pag. 619, 620, 621.

(†) *Campian* justly executed for High Treason 24 of *Eliz.* 1581. Vide *Camden's Elizab.* Lib. 3. pag. 239, 240.

(*) *MARTYR CHRISTI INCLYTUS, & sui seculi CLA-RISSIMUS.* Pet. Ribadeneira in Catalogo Scriptorum, Religionis Societatis Jesu, in Edmundo Campiano. *Parsons* the Jesuite says as much for *Garnet*, in his Discussion of the Answer of *W. B.* pag. 22, 23.

of their *(a) Authors*, writing againſt King *James*, (of happy Memory) tells us,

1. That *the Pope's Power (in the* BELIEF *of* CATHOLICKS*) is not barely Miniſterial, but* IMPERIAL. CATHOLICI (ſays he) *non tantum* MINISTERIO, *ſed &* IMPERIO *Papam præſidere* CREDUNT. And this Papal Power is *(b)* SUPREME, *ſo that there reſides in the Pope a Right to direct and* COMPEL, *and a* POWER *of* LIFE AND DEATH. And to ſhew the reaſon of this, he adds; *(c) That the* POPE *is the* SUPREME VICAR *of* GOD, *the Emperor Supreme* ADVOCATE *of the Church, than which* NOTHING *can be more* HONOU-RABLE *for any* KING : (Surely Kings are much bound to him for that Honourable Office.) *The* POPE (as he goes on) *is* THE HEAD *of Chriſt's Body; The Emperor and Kings are* ARMS *and* HANDS : *And therefore it is* MADNESS *to ſay, That the* HEAD *has not* EMPIRE *over the* ARMS. *The Pope, who is the Head and Top of the Eccleſiaſtical Body,is govern'd by the* INSPIRATION *of the Holy Ghoſt. The* ARMS *can do nothing, but what pertains to the Food, Rayment, and Protection of the Body. And St. Paul forbids us to doubt, that the Government and Preſcription of all theſe, belongs to the Head, and from thence is derived to the* ARMS. *And therefore if Kings do not feed and cloath the Body, if the* ARMS *or* HANDS *do not do their Office, they may (by the Command of the* HEAD*) be* CUT OFF, *as unprofitable*

(a) Gaſp. Scioppius, *In his* Ecceſiaſticum Jacobo Magnæ Britanniæ Regi Oppoſitum, cap.137. pag.302. Edit. 1611.

(b) Penes Papam in Eccleſia SUMMUM IMPERIUM, *Poteſtas* SUMMA, *tam dirigenti quam* COGENDI, *ſu etiam* VIT. *&* NECIS *reſidet.* Ib.dem, cap.138. pag. 456.

(c) Papa eſt SUMMUS DEI VICARIUS, *Cæſar ſummus Eccleſiæ* ADVOCATUS; *quo* NIHIL ULLI REGI *amplius, aut* HONORIFICENTIUS. *Papa* CAPUT *eſt Corporis Chriſti, Cæſar ac* REGES *ſunt* BRACHIA *ſeu* MANUS. *Itaque inſania eſt dicere, nullum Caput in Brachia imperium eſſe. Papa qui eſt Caput & vertex Eccleſiaſtici corporis) Spiritus a ni ſi inſpiratione regitur.* BRACHIA NIHIL *facere poſſunt, niſi quod ad corperis Victum, amictum ac protectionem pertinet ; quorum omnium Regimen ac preſcriptum, quin penes Caput ſit, & inde ad Brachia derivetur, Dubitare Paulus vetat.* Col.2.19. *Itaque ſi Reges non nutriant, neque veſtiant Corpus.* — *Si Brachii aut Manus munere non fungantur, nec teneant Caput.* — *Ut membrum inutile,* CAPITIS IMPERIO AMPUTENTUR. Ibid. Cap. 241. pag. 511. If you deſire to ſee more of the Pope's Depoſing Kings, Card. *Baronius* (in an hundred places) vindicates the Power, and approves and commends the practice. See his Annals *ad Annum* 593. num. 8. *& ad Annum* 730. num. 5.

unprofitable Members. These are his words, or the English of them.

So that (by this Popish Doctrine) the Pope, being Head of the Body, may, when he pleases, (for he is Supreme and Sole Judge in the case) cut off Kings and Emperors, who are but the Hands or Arms of that Body. And yet so hard is the Forehead of that Author, that he is not ashamed to say, (and put it in the Margent, that all might take notice of it) *That this great Power of the Pope, is* (d) *NOT AT ALL dangerous or prejudicial to Princes.* How dangerous this Doctrine of this Papal Supremacy, has been to Princes, the many Excommunications and Depositions of Kings and Emperors, in the six last Centuries, are evident and sad Witnesses; and what mischief (if not carefully prevented) it may do for the future, it will concern Princes, and all who are Loyal, and love Them, and their own Preservation, seriously to consider. It was a Wise-Man's saying, That Protestant Princes may be too secure, but never safe, while any Jesuite dwells in their Dominions. *Thuanus* speaking of the fatal, and (by them, too secure) not fear'd Tragedy of *Hen.* 3. and 4. of *France,* he seems to blame their too great Security, and then adds: *MISEROS PRINCIPES, QUIBUS DE CONJURATIONE NON CREDITUR, NISI OCCISIS.* But to proceed.

(d) *Summa Papæ potestas NIHIL PRORSUS PERICULI ADFERT REGIBUS.* Idem cap. 141. pag. 512.

2. Another of their Authors, and he a Learned Bishop, (*Jacobus* (e) *Simanca* by Name) tells us that, which concerns all Protestant Princes to consider, and what they must expect from the

(e) Jacobus Simanca Enchir. Judicum, Tit. 67, Sect. 12. pag. 349. Antwerp. 1573. *HÆRETICI PRIVATI SUNT OMNI DOMINIO & Jurisdictione, & EORUM SUBITI ab eis LIBERI sunt, quod & REGES, & alios rerum Dominos comprehendit.*

the Pope, when he has Power to put their Trayterous Principles in execution. The thing he tells us, is this: *Heretiques* (says he, and we know who are meant by that hard word) *are actually DEPRIVED of ALL DOMINION and JURISDICTION, and their SUBJECTS FREED FROM THEIR OBEDIENCE: and this comprehends KINGS, and OTHER LORDS.* So *Simanca*. Nor is this his private or singular Opinion: For, 1. He proves it expresly out of a Decretal of Pope *Gregory* the Ninth, extant in the Body of their (*f*) Canon-Law. 2. He cites (*g*) *Alphonsus à Castro*, who also proves the Position of *Simanca*, by evident Testimonies of many and eminent Popish Authors. 3. It is to be considered too, that *Simanca's* Book is Priviledg'd, and Licenc'd to be Printed by Publick Authority, and with the Approbation and high Commendation of the *Censor Librorum*, the Learned *Ben. Arias Montanus*; who tells us, that he had read it, (*h*) And judged it HIGHLY PROFITABLE, for the Knowledge and PRACTICE of the WHOLE Argument undertaken, and that it contain'd NOTHING OFFENSIVE to the CATHOLICK FAITH, (then, in that great Man's Judgment, that Rebellious Roman Doctrine, of Deposing Heretical Kings, and Absolving their Subjects from all Oaths of Allegiance, is not offensive to their Catholick Faith.) And therefore I JUDGE it WORTHY, that FOR THE PROFIT OF MANY, it be A THIRD TIME

(*f*) Cap. Absolutos 16. Extra. *de Hæreticis*.

(*g*) Alph. à Castro, *de Justâ Hæreticor. Punit.* Lib. 2. Cap. 7. &c.

(*h*) *Valde utilem esse censeo ad TOTIUS argumenti suscepti cognitionem, & PRAXIM, NIHILQUE continere quod CATHOLICAM FIDEM offendat; ideoque DIGNUM judico, ut ad MULTORUM UTILITATEM, TERTIO, & etiam SÆPIUS edatur:* So are the words in *Arias Montanus* his Licence of that Book.

TIME, and *OFTNER*, *Publiſhed*. So that this *Doctrine*, (That Heretical *Kings* are Depriv'd of all their Dominion, and their *Subjects* Abſolved from all Oaths of Allegiance) is *not only* approved by *Simanca*, *Alfonſus à Caſtro*, *Arias Montanus*, (all great and very learned *Perſons* in the *Church of Rome*) but by their Canon-Law, and the Decretal of Pope *Gregory* the Ninth. And it is further conſiderable, that this Doctrine (though Impious and Trayterous) is not (in any *Index Expurgatorius*, I have yet ſeen) condemned either in *Simanca*, or any other of all thoſe, who generally aſſert and vindicate it.

3. One more I ſhall only cite, (though an hundred ſuch might be cited) and he a famous *Jeſuite*, who plainly tells us, (what their Society conſtantly *profeſs*, and *many of them have, and do practice*) (i) *That if a CLERGY-MAN Rebel againſt his KING, it is NO TREASON, becauſe CLERGY-MEN are not the KINGS SUBJECTS.* Nor is this the ſingular Opinion of *Emanuel Sa*; for it is *approved*, and highly *commended* (by their *Cenſores Librorum*) both at the (k) *beginning*, and (l) *end* of that Book; and (as an (m) excellent and learned Perſon tells me) it was highly approved and commended at *Rome* too. So that (if ſuch a multitude of eminent Popiſh Authors may have that credit they deſerve in this particular) we may be ſure, that this impious and trayterous Doctrine is approved and received

(i) *Clerici rebellio in Regem, non eſt crimen læſæ Majeſtatis, quia Clericus non eſt Regi Subditus.* Eman. Sa, Aphor. Confeſſ. Verbo Clericus, pag. 41. Col. 1599.

(k) *Opus Theologis, OMNIBUSQUE animarum curam habentibus UTILE ac NECESSARIUM.*

(l) *Hi Aphoriſmi DOCTI ſunt ac PII, MULTAMQUE Utilitatem allaturi.*

(m) Jac. Leſchaſſier operum pag. 421. Edit. Paris 1652.

ceived in the Church of *Rome*. And though I said I would cite no more such Testimonies, to manifest so certain and clear a Truth; yet I shall add two more, (not unworthy your Consideration) which are (if that be possible) more highly impious than the former.

1. Then, a great Popish (*n*) Lawyer, (in asserting the Papal Power) has, and endeavours to prove these erroneous and desperate Positions.

(*n*) Phil. Maynardus de Privilegiis Ecclesiast. Dedicated to Pope *Paulus* 5. and printed at *Ancona* 1607.

(1) *Imperator subest Papæ, ut & Reges*, Art. 5. Sect. 19. 21.

1. *The Emperour and Kings are the Popes Subjects.*

(2) *Imperator & Rex ratione fidei & peccati gravis, possunt a Papa deponi & privari,* Ibid. Sect. 23.

2. *The Emperor and Kings may be Deposed by the Pope, for Heresie and any great Sin.*

(3) *Papa habet potestatem in toto Orbe, in Spiritualibus & Temporalibus; & in Temporalibus modo digniori, superiori, & perfectiori quam habent Principes seculares,* Ibid. Art. 6. Sect. 1. & Sect. 11.

3. *The Pope has Power in the whole World, in Spirituals and* TEMPORALS; *and this* TEMPORAL *Power he has in a more Worthy, a Superiour and perfect manner, than Secular Princes.*

(4) *Statuta Laicorum non obligant Clericos,* Art. 13. Sect. 9.

4. *Statutes made by Laymen, do not bind the Clergy.*

(5) *Vicarius Dei Omnibus Potestatibus præponitur,* SICUT IPSE DEUS, & PAPÆ SUBJECT OMNIS CREATURA, Ibid. Art. 6. Sect. 11. 12.

5. *The Pope is Vicar of God, and Preferred before all Powers, as* GOD. HIMSELF; *and* EVERY CREATURE IS SUBJECT TO HIM.

(6) *Papæ subesse, est* DE NECESSITATE SALUTIS, & *contrarium asserens,* NON POTES DICI CHRISTIANUS. Ibidem Sect. 13.

6. *It is necessary to Salvation to be Subject to the Pope, and he who affirms the contrary,* IS NO CHRISTIAN.

(*o*) Cap. Unam Sanct. De Major. & Obedientia. Int. Extrav. Communes.

This he has out of the (*o*) Canon-Law, and the Decretal of Pope *Boniface* the Eight. So that by this impious and uncharitable Doctrine, all *Protestant Kings, Princes* and *People*, are deny'd to be *Christians*, and *absolutely damned*, without all hope or possibility of *Salvation*.
And

And yet their *(p) Canonists* (to say nothing of others) and *(q) Jesuites* generally, (nay, *(r)* universally) approve and defend it, and the Pope and *(s) Council* confirm and establish it. *Theologia hæc damnatoria, Pseudo-Catholica, Romana sit licet, tamen non est Christiana.* Let them brag (as usually they do) of their *Catholick Faith*; for my part, I can have no great Opinion of their Faith, who have little Charity, and damn all save themselves.

2. Once more, *(t) Stanislaus Ozichovius* (while he magnifies the Pope and his Papal Greatness, with high contempt of Kings, and Blasphemy against God) hath this passage, unfit to fall from the Pen of any sober Christian, *(u) The PRIEST* (says he) *excels THE KING, as much as a MAN excels a BEAST.* And says further, *HE WHO PREFERS THE KING BEFORE THE PRIEST, he prefers the CREATURE before the CREATOR.* This is strange Doctrine, and yet approved at *Rome,* at least not condemned there, (as Antimonarchical Positions, which decry Royal, and magnifie Papal Power, seldom, or never are) the reason why I say and believe this, is; Because I find in the *(x) Spanish Expurgatory Index,* some other things of *this Author* censur'd; but this passage now cited, is neither medl'd with, nor once mention'd.

But to pass by particular Testimonies of single Popish Authors, (who publickly assert, and industriously

(p) Vid. Glossam ad dictum Cap. Unam Sanctam & Card. Turrecrematam summa de Ecclesiâ, Lib. 4. Part 1. Pag. 409.
(q) Vid. Bellarmin. de Pont. Rom. Lib. 5. cap. 7. Sect. Item. & Sect. sic enim.
(r) Vid. Apologiam Jesuitarum, Editam Anno 1595 cum hoc Titulo *La verité defendue,*
(s) Vid. Sanction. Pragmat. (Paris 1613. in Quarto) pag. 1042. & Concil. Lateran. sub Leone 10. Sess. 11. apud Binium, Tom. 9. Concil. pag. 155. A And that *OBEDIENTIA VERA* (and so *Subjection*) is due and to be given *Jesu Christi Vicario Pontifici Romano,* is an Article of their NEW CREED, (contrived at Trent) *EXTRA QUAM NULLUS SALVUS ESSE POTEST* ; and to the belief of this, all their Ecclesiasticks solemnly swear. Vid. Bullam *Pii 4.* super Forma Professionis Fidei, in Concilio Tridentino Sess. 25.
(t) Stanislaus Ozichovius in Chimæra, pag. 99.
(u) Sacerdos præstat Regi Quantum HOMO præstat BESTIÆ. Qui Regem præfert Sacerdoti, ii CREATUR. IM anteponit CREATORI, loco citato.

(x) Index Expurgatorius Hispan. in Stanislao Ozichovio.

ously endeavour to Vindicate this Rebellious Doctrine, *That Kings may be depofed and murdered by the Pope or People.*) I shall give you greater, and (to the Church of *Rome*) more Authentique Authority. As for instance,

1. Their (*y*) *Canon-Law*, approved, received, used and obey'd in their Church, as a Rule of Justice in all their Courts and Consistories. I shall quote their best Edition; Corrected, Approved, and Publish'd by the Popes Command, (and he Infallible no doubt) for so he himself tells us........(*z*) *Nos providere volentes, ut hoc Jus Canonicum, sic EXPURGATUM, ad OMNES CHRISTI FIDELES SARTUM perveniat, ac ne cuiquam liceat operi QUICQUAM ADDERE, vel IMMUTARE, aut INVERTERE, sed prout in urbe nostra Romà nuper impressum fuit, perpetuo integrum & INCORRUPTUM construetur.* Now in his Canon-Law, so *purged* and *corrected*, that it might come to *ALL THE FAITHFUL*, (as the *Pope himself tells us*, who, if he were infallible could not, and if he were but an honest man, would not publish an untruth) we are told,

I. That the Pope may depose Princes, and then absolve their Subjects from their Oathes of Allegiance (*a*)......*A FIDELITATIS etiam JURAMENTO, Romanus Pontifex nonnullos ABSOLVIT, cum aliquos A SUA DIGNITATE DEPONIT.* And having set down this for Law, it immediately follows,

II. That

(*y*) Decretum Gratiani E-*MENDATUM*, jussu Gregorii. 13. Editum, juxta, Exemplar *ROMANUM, DILIGENTER RECOGNITUM.* Paris. 1612.

(*z*) Gregorius Papa 13. in Bulla Corpori Juris Canonici præfixâ Dat. Romæ. 1580. Anno Pontificatus sui. 9.

(*a*) Vid. Can. Authoritatem. 2. Causs. 15. Quæst. 6. Part. 2.

II. That (b) another Pope (*Zachary* by name) deposed the King of France; *not so much for HIS INIQUITIES; but that he was UNPROFITABLE for such a power......And then he ABSOLVED ALL THE FRENCH from their Oath of FIDEDITY*; And then adds......*That the Holy-Church* (he meanes the Pope) *does* (by an usual authority) *so absolve Subjects from their Oathes to their Superiors.*

(b) *Alius autem Rom. Pontifex, Zacharias scilicet, Regem Francorum, non tam pro sua Iniquitatibus; quam pro eo, quod tantæ potestati erat inutilis, à REGNO DEPOSUIT, cm. nesque Francigenos à JURAMENTO FIDELITATIS, quod illi fecerunt, ABSOLVIT: Quod etiam ex AUTHORITATE FREQUENTI fecit Ecclesia.* Ibid. Can. Alius 3.

Now concerning this *memorable Canon*, give me leave to observe,

1. That the Gloss tells us (*John Semeca*, a famous Canonist, was Author of it) that Pope *Gelasius* maintain'd the doctrine of deposing Emperors (c) ....*Gelasius Papa scribens contra Anastasium Imperatorem, dicit, QUOD POTEST EUM DEPONERE PROPTER malitiam suam*, &c.

(c) Gloss ad dictum Canonem. verbo *Alius*.

2. In the *Lemma*, or *Title* of this *Canon* (in the (d) old *Editions* of the Canon-Law) It was ......*Gelasius Papa Anastasio Imporatori.* But in *later* (e) *Editions* the Title is this......... *Pontificalis Authoritas A JURAMENTO FIDELITATIS nonnullos ABSOLVIT, unde Gregorius Papa.* The (f) Annotator tells us truly; that *Gelasius* could not speak of the French Kings deposition; seeing *Gelasius* was dead, above 240 years before *Chilpericus* (or *Childericus*, they write him both wayes) came

(d) Edit. Parif. 1519, &c.

(e) Edit. Lugduni. 1664, &c.

(f) Vid. Notam ad dictum Can. *Alius*; in Edit. recentioribus.

came to be King of *France*. But they say, the words of this Canon are found in the (*g*) *Epistles* of Pope *Gregory* the Seventh, and therefore they do rightly refer them to him, as the true Author of them. Now, whether it were *Gelasius*, or *Gregory* the Seventh, it is all one, (as to my present business) it is by them confess'd, that a Pope was Author of that *Rebellious passage*, *Gratian* refers it into the *Body* of their *Canon-Law*, and Pope (*h*) *Gregory* the Thirteenth approves, and (together with the whole Body of the Law, the Gloss and Annotations) confirmes and ratifies it. Whence we may rationally conclude, that this doctrine, of the *Popes power to depose Kings*, and *absolve their subjects from their Oathes of Allegiance* (though impious and rebellious) is so far from being *disown'd*, or *detested by all Papists* (as some now pretend) that the Supreme power of that Church has not onely approved, but establish'd it for Law. By the way; though you see, that *Gratian* and Pope *Gregory* say, that Pope *Zachary* was the Man who deposed the French King *Hildericus*; yet (*i*) *an Historian* of more Antiquity and Credit than either of them (notwithstanding *Gregories* Infallibility) tells us, that it was Pope *Stephen* (*Zacharies* Successor) who *deposed him*. So that all agree, that *A Pope* (it matters not which) was Author of that impiety.

(*g*) Gregorius. 7. Regist. lib. 8. Epist. 21.

(*b*) Vide Bullam Gregorii. 13. Dat. Romæ. 1. Julii, 1580. Corpori Jur. Can. præfixam.

(*i*) Eginhardus in Vitâ Caroli Magni, p. 4, 5. Edit Colon. 1521. who sayes...... *Hildericus Rex, JUSSU STEPHANI, Romani Pontificis, depositus est*. This impious Fact of Pope *Stephen*, has been approv'd, and (in practice) imitated by many of his followers. *Bzovius* (before cited) gives us a list of above 30 Kings and Princes, thus deposed by Popes, and Anathematiz'd.

3. When

3. When the Canon fayes, that the French King was depofed by the Pope, becaufe he was *INVTILIS*, &c. the Glofs gives you the meaning of that word; ......*Non intelligas*, *INVTILIS*, *id eft INSVFFICIENS*, *tunc enim ei dari debuit Coadjutor*; *fed quia DISSOLVTVS erat, cum* (†) *MVLIERIBVS*, *& EFFOEMINATVS*; fo that (by this Papal Law) we fee, that (if the Pope pleafe) the greateft Prince may be depofed for a very fmall matter.

(†) *Ipfe Papa Pater Patrum putativus, fed filiorum I'ERVS Pater: quod, qui Nepotes ejus, omnes norunt.* Il N. potifmo, pag.——

4. When this Canon fayes ; the *Pope depofed the King* of *France*; the (*k*) *Glofs* notes .....*Ergo Papa deponit Imperatorem*. And (leaft we fhould not take notice of it) thefe words (in their beft Editions of the Canon-Laws (*l*) corrected, purged, revifed, and whatever wicked men had put into the Text or Margent, contrary to the Catholick Faith, by Pope Gregories command, expunged) I fay (notwithftanding all this) thefe words are put in the Margent ......*IMPERATOR POTEST A PAPA DEPONI*. Whence it is evident, that in Pope Gregories Opinion, this *impious doctrine* and Pofition (though contrary to the *true Chriftian*) is not contrary to *THEIR ROMAN FAITH*; being exprefly in thofe Gloffes and Canons; in which, their Supreme and Infallible Judge fayes, There is *NOTHING CATHOLICÆ VERITATI CONTRARIVM.* Nor is this Pope *Gregories* fingular opinion ; that the Pope may depofe Kings. For feeing

(*k*) Gloffa ad dictum, Cau. *Alius.* 3. Verbo, depofuit.

(*l*) *Cum his quæ ab impiis Scriptoribus, extra in margine, vel intra afperfa fuerunt Catholicæ veritati contraria revidendi, corrigendi, expurgandi curam demandavimus......JAM TOTVM EMENDATVM*, &c. In Bullâ dictâ Gregorii 13.

it

it has been approved by their *Popes*, and their *General Councils* (as you shall see anon) and for some ages received amongst their *Sacred Canons* (as they call them) it is become a necessary part of their *Creed* (and *no salvation* without the beliefe of it) to which all their *Secular Clergy*, *Archbishops*, *Bishops*, and whoever *has any Cure of Souls*; and all their *Regulars* (at least the *Heads and Governors of them*) are solemnly (*m*) Sworn. For they swear, promise, and vow, without all doubtings, to receive, and profess ALL THINGS defined and declared in the SACRED CANONS, and General Councils; and (so far as they are able) to make others receive them too. So that all their Ecclesiastiques (especially all who have any Cure of Souls) do not onely believe this *impious doctrine* of *Popes power to depose Kings*, but they Swear, both to BELIEVE and PROFESS IT, and (as far as they are able) make others do so too. How pernicious to Kings and Princes, such Principles, and such persons (Sworn to Profess and Promote them) heretofore have been; the many sad and Tragical examples of deposed Princes, in the six last Centuries, can abundantly witness, and assure us: And how pernicious (for the future) they may be, unless (with care and prudence) they be prevented, we, or our posterity may unhappily, and too soon see. *Dirum omen! miserecors, qui solus potest, averruncet Deus.*

(*m*) One Article of the Trent-Creed is this....*Item OMNIA à Sacris CANONIBUS & Oecumenicis Conciliis definita, INDUBITANTER recipio & profiteor....Hanc Catholicam fidem, extra quam non est SALUS profiteor, & ab ALIIS teneri, (quantum in me est) curabo.* Ita habent verba Professionis fidei, in Bullâ dictâ Pii Papæ. 4. Concil. Tridentin. sess. 25.

5. Lastly,

5. Laftly; If we confult Cardinal (*n*) *Turrecremata* (a very great and learned perfon) who well underftood their facred Canons, and in what fenfe the Roman Church received them) he, in his Commentary on the Canon before-cited, affirmes, and endeavours to prove thefe following (*o*) Propofitions.

(*n*) Johan. Card. de Turrecremata, ad Can. Alius 3. Cauf. 15 Quæft. 6. & in fumma de Ecclefia, lib. 2. cap. 14, &c.

(*o*) The Cardinals own words are thefe which follow,

I. *The Pope may DEPOSE the Emperor, or a King not fubject to the Emperor.*
II. *The Pope may LAWFULLY abfolve Subjects from their Oath of Allegiance.*
III. *The Pope may depofe Counts, Dukes, and other Barons, without the Confent of the Emperor, or thofe Kings, whofe fubjects they are.*
IV. *Subjects (if they have the Popes confent) which they are fure to have (if it make for his intereft) may depofe their Kings.* This he farther proves, and adds.....*That if the King be a manifeft Heretick* (as all Proteftants are with them) *then THE CHURCH may depofe him.*

I. Papa poteft deponere Imperatorem, aut Regem, qui non fubjeft Imperatori.

II. Papa LICITE poteft abfolvere fubditos a juramento fidelitatis.

III. Papa poteft deponere Comites, Duces & alios Barones, fine confenfu Imperatorum, aut Regum quibus fubfunt.

IV. Subditi (fi habeant affenfum Papæ) poffunt Regem deponere.....Et fi Rex fit manifeftus HÆRETICUS, poteft ab Ecclefia deponi.

The Premifes confider'd, it will highly concern all Proteftant Kings and Princes to look to it, who (as Hereticks) are all damned, and (*p*) Anathematiz'd once every year, on *Maundy-Thurfday*, in their *Bulla Cœnæ Domini.* For, had they of *Rome* power to act according to their Principles, Pretences, and Intereft, they would make fhort work, a fpeedy and thorough Reformation; and compel all Proteftant (or as they conftantly mifcall them, Heretical)

(*p*) Vid. Bullam dictam à Clemente X. Editam, An. 1671. 7. Cal. April. & Pontif. fui An. 1. In Bullario Rom. Lugduni, 1673. P. 528. Sect. 1.

Heretical) Kings and Princes, to quit their Religion, or their Realms and Kingdomes.

Be it concluded then; that (according to the Approved and Received Doctrine of the *Roman Church*) *Kings* and *Princes* may be *deposed*, and their *subjects absolved* from their *Oaths of Allegiance*. And for the truth of what I here say; we have *the Precept and Practice of three Popes* (*Zachary, Gregory the Seventh*, and *Urban the Second*) and *three* (*q*) *Canons* grounded on that *Papal authority*, received into the Body *of their Canon-Law*: which, when you have occasion, you may (for further satisfaction) consult.

Now if you inquire, *for what Crimes* Kings may be deposed by the Pope; whether for *Heresie* onely (for thats universally agreed on) or for other Crimes also? *John Semeca* (Author of the Gloss on *Gratian*) gives us *a full and Categorical Answer.* For 1. He (*r*) proposes the Question: *Pro quo peccato potest Imperator deponi?* For what *Sin can the Emperor be depofed?* (That he may be deposed, is (in that Law) no Question, but an undoubted truth; the Question onely is, for what Crimes it may be done.) And the Answer is ......(*s*) *That he may be deposed for ANY SIN, if he be INCORRIGIBLE; and not onely for his sins, but if he* (*t*) *UNPROFITABLIE manage that Regal Power:* And this he proves out of another Canon. This is the *sad condition* of *Kings and Emperors* (by the Popish *Canon-Law*) they may be deposed (if they be *incorrigible*) for *ANY SIN*, and sometimes for *no sin*; at least as the *principal cause of their deposition.* Whereas (by the *same Law*)

(*q*) Vide Gratian. Can. *Alius*. 3 Can. *Nos Sanctorum.* 4. & Can. *Juratos*, 5. Cauſ. 15. Quæſt. 6.

(*r*) Gloſſa ad *Can. ſi Papa.* 6. Diſt. 40. Verbo. *A fide devius.*

(*s*) *PRO QUOLIBET peccato poteſt Imperator deponi, ſi ſit incorrigibilis.* Ibidem.
(*t*) *Papa Zacharias Regem Francorum, non tam pro ſuis iniquitatibus, quam quod tantæ poteſtati erat INUTILIS, depoſuit.* Can. Alius. 2. Cauſ. 15. Quæſt. 6.

Law) if the *Pope* be so (*u*) *prodigiously impious*, that he not onely damn himself, but carry [*IN-NUMERABILES POPULOS*] *innumerable people to hell with him*, yet there is *no deposing*, or *Judging him*. This not only the *Canon in Gratian*, but a long *Annotation* (lately added, since *Gratians* time) *approves*, and *confirmes*: and *Pope Gregory* the Thirteenth *approves* both the *Canon*, and *Annotation*, in his (*x*) Bull, I have so often mention'd. So that (according to this Law) If the Emperor, or any King, will not be good Boyes, and *obey their Grand Maister* (*Dominum DEUM NOSTRUM*, as they call him) the Pope; if they will not *be corrected by him*, and amend what he thinks amiss (for he is *Supreme* and *Sole Judge* of the *Crime* and *punishment*) Then the *Pope may*, and (if he have ability and opportunity, we may be sure) *he will depose them*.

(*u*) Dicto Can. Si Papa. 6. Dist. 40.

(*x*) Bulla Gregorii. 13 Corp. Jur. Can. præfixa.

Thus much (and may be too much) for the Canon-Law; that Sink of Forgeries, Impiety, and Disloyalty. For I scarce know any Book, wherein are more forged writings (under good names sometimes) for bad purposes; or more Impious Doctrines and Positions own'd and authoriz'd for Law, and that by one who pretends (though without, and against all reason) to be *Christ's* Vicar, and Infallible; or any Book which has more Seditious and Rebellious *Principles of Disloyalty*. This I onely say now, but when I have (what now I want) time, and opportunity; I can, and (Σὺν Θεῷ) will make it good. How dangerous, and (when believ'd

[36]   Popish Principles, &c

believ'd and practis'd) how pernicious to Kings and Princes, the Principles of that Law are, you may (in part) see by the premises: if you desire more, you may (at your leasure) consult, and consider those Places here *mention'd in the Margent* (*a*) with the Glosse and Case upon them; together with Cardinal *Turrecremata*'s Commentary on *Gratian*'s Decree, and *Panormitan* on the Decretals (to omit all other Canonists (you will find Evidence, more than enough, to convince you, out of their own Testimonies, that the Principles of their own Law, as explain'd by their greatest, and best Interpreters, are not onely Dangerous, but Destructive of the Right of Kings, and inconsistent with that Loyalty, which (by the Laws of *Nature* and *Scripture*) are really due to them.

3. But besides these Testimonies of *particular Writers* of their own Church, and their Approved, and (by Publick Authority) Establish'd, and *Receiv'd Canon-Law*, we have greater and more *Authentick Testimonies*, that in the Popish Church, they both *profess and practice* this impious and rebellious doctrine, of *Anathematizing*, and *Deposing Kings and Emperors*, of giving away their Kingdoms to others, and *Absolving their Subjects* from their *Oathes of Allegiance* and *Fidelity*. For their Popes (who are their Supreme and Infallible Judges) testifie as much, in their *Breves* and *Bulls*; and those not forged, or corrupted by *Hereticks*; but Publish'd by themselves, and Printed at *Rome*, in their

---

(*a*) Vide Gratian: Dist. 96. in Lemmate, & Can. 1.7,8,9,10,11. Cujus Lemma est, *Quod Imperatores debent Pontificibus SUBESSE, non PRÆESSE.* Can. etiam 11. Can. etiam.1.,3,4,5. Caus. 15. Quæst. 6. & Can. *Excommunicatorum,* 47. Caus. 23. Quæst. 5. & cap. Vergentis 10. & cap. Excommunic. 13. & cap. absolutos. 16. Extra De Hæreticis, & cap. *Gravem.* 13. Extra de Pœnis.& cap. *Ad Apostolic.* 1. De sent. & re Judicata, in 6, & 7. Decret. lib 2. Tit. 1. cap. 1. Cujus Lemma est. *LAICIS in Clericos NULLA POTESTAS* & 7. Decret. lib. 2. Tit. 2. cap. 2. & ibidem lib. 5. Tit. 3. *De Hæreticis & Schismaticis*, cap. 9. &c. Et cap. *Nimis* 30. Extra *De Jurejurando*. Cujus Lemma est, *Clerici non tenentur Laicis præstare Juramenta FIDELITATIS,* & cap. *Solicitæ.* 6. Extra, *De Major. & Obedientia.*

their own (z) *Vatican Press.* Where (to omit others) we have,

1. The *Bull of Pius the Fifth* against Queen Elizabeth. The *Title* prefixed to that impious Bull, is this: (a) *DAMNATIO, & Excommunicatio Elizabethæ, Reginæ Angliæ, eique ADHÆRENTIUM.* Where (in one breath and *Bull*) he Damns that *Innocent Queen,* and all her Loyal Subjects, (*Protestants* and *Papists.*) Where (by the way) it is to be considered, That if *any Papists* be Loyal, (as by the *Law of God and Nature* they ought) to any *Heretical King or Prince,* (and at *Rome,* our Gracious King, and all Protestants are such) it is *reputed their Crime,* and *they Damn'd at Rome for it.* For it is not only (OMNES (b) *& SINGULOS HÆRETICOS, QUICCUNQUE NOMINE CENSEANTUR*) All and singular Heretiques, of what sort soever, but also all those, *who RECEIVE, FAVOUR or DEFEND them.* So that if any *Roman-Catholick Favour,* or (according to his *Natural,* or *Sworn Allegiance*) *Defend* his *Prince,* who is a *Protestant,* (and so a *Declared Heretique*) he is under the same *Anathema* and *Condemnation.* And this *Anathema* and *Condemnation* of *all Heretiques,* and *all those* who *Favour* or *Defend them,* is solemnly renewed every (c) year at *Rome,* and lately referred into the Body of their (d) *Canon-Law.*

But to proceed: In this Bull of Pope *Pius the Fifth,* which contains the Anathema and Damnation (as 'tis called in the *Lemma* prefix'd to that Bull) of Queen *Elizabeth;* which proved *BRUTUM FULMEN,*

(z) Vid. Bullarium Romanum, per Cherubinum Romæ ex Typograph. Cameræ Apostolicæ. Anno 1638.

(a) Dicti Bullarii, Tom. 1. pag. 229. and in the Edition at Lions, Anno 1655. pag. 303. It is dated 5. Cal. Maii. 1570. Elizabethæ Anno 13. Till which year all Papists came to our Common-prayers.

(b) Vide Bullam Clementis 10. dat. Romæ, 7. Cal. April. 1671. in Bullario Cherubini Lugduni 1673. Tom. 5. Pag. 526.

(c) In Bulla Cænæ Domini.
(d) Vide 7. Decret. lib. 5. Tit. 3. cap. 2, & 9. pag. 192. & 203. Edit. Lugd. 1661.

FULMEN, (the good and moſt gratious GOD bleſſing what the Pope impiouſly curſed) we have theſe Particulars very conſiderable.

1. The extravagant Power the Pope aſſumes; when he tells us, That our Bleſſed Saviour did *Conſtitute Peter*, and by conſequence (e) *Him*, (as St. *Peter's* Succeſſor.).... *SUPER OMNES GENTES, & OMNIA Regna PRINCIPEM, ut EVELLAT, DESTRUAT, DISSIPET, DISPERDAT, &c.* Theſe are the words of *God* to (f) *Jeremy*, (not *Peter* or his Succeſſors) miſerably miſunderſtood and miſapplyed by *this Pope* and (g) *his Predeceſſors*. Here is a pretence to a *vaſt* and *deſtructive Power*; and though it be a bare pretence, and (without any juſt ground) irrational and ridiculous; yet let Princes look to it. For when the Popes had Power, they did; and when they have, they will make uſe of it.

2. This premiſed, he proceeds to his Damnatory Sentence, in theſe words: (h) *We* (faith he) *by the Plenitude of Apoſtolical Power, declare the ſaid* Elizabeth *an Heretick, and both her, and her Adherents, to have incurr'd the Sentence of Excommunication, and to be all cut off from the Unity of the Body of Chriſt*. But this is not all; He proceeds (very unlike à *Chriſtian*, and what he would be *thought*, Chriſt's Vicar) to Depoſe her, from all her Royal Dignity, and all that Dominion, to which ſhe had (by Birth,

---

(c) *Chriſtus — QUI NOS in hoc SUPREMO JUSTITIÆ THRONO voluit collocare.* Dictæ Bullæ. Sect. 3.

(f) Jer. 1. 10.

(g) By *Innocent.* 3. and yet it goes for Law. Cap. *Solicitæ.* 6. Extra *De Major. & Obed.* and by *Boniface* the 8. cap. *Unam Sanctam* 8. codem Tit. *Extravag.* Com. &c.

(h) *Nos Apoſtolicæ poteſtatis plenitudine declaramus, prædictam Elizabetham Hæreticâ eique adhærentes, Anathematis ſententiam incurriſſe, eſſeque A CHRISTI CORPORIS UNITATE PRÆCISOS.* Dictæ Bullæ Sect. 3.

Birth, the Law of God, and the Land) a juſt Right, in the following Form ----

3. *And we* (i) *Deprive her of her pretended Royal Right, and all Dominion, Dignity and Priviledge whatſoever.* He calls it, Her PRE- TENDED Royal Right, becauſe (according to their Rebellious and Impious Principles) ſhe being an Heretick, (as they miſcall'd her) for that Crime ſhe had loſt her Royal Right, even before her actual Excommunication. Nor is this all; he proceeds.----

(i) *Quinetiam ipſam pretenſo REGNI JURE, nec non OM- NI & quocunque DOMINIO, DIGNITATE, privilegioque PRIVATAM.* Ibid. Sect. 4.

4. *And further,* (k) *we Abſolve all the Nobility, Subjects, and People* of England, *and all others who have any way Sworn to her, from ſuch Oath; and we declare them FOR EVER Abſolved from any Obligation of Allegiance or Obedience to her; and we do (by theſe Preſents) Abſolve them.* So that here, (ſo far as was able) he Abſolves all her Subjects, from the Obligation of the Oaths, in which they had ſworn Allegiance. But becauſe there is, (as the Lawyers truly ſay) A Natural, as well as *A Sworn Allegiance*; (for, by Birth, they who never ſwore it, owe a Natural Allegiance to their Prince, being born Subjects) left, (after their Oath was null'd) they ſhould Obey the Queen, and (upon the Principle of Natural Allegiance) think themſelves bound ſo to do; He goes on, to declare this Natural Bond Null, and frees them from any Obligation of it: Thus :----

(k) *Item Proceres, ſubditos & populos dicti Regni, ac cæteros OMNES, qui illi QUOMO- DOCUNQUE JURAVE- RUNT, à JURAMENTO hu- juſmodi, ac OMNI prorſus do- minii, fidelitatis & obſequii de- bito perpetuo abſolutos, & præ- ſenti authoritate abſolvimus* Ibid. Sect. 5.

5. *We* (l) *Command, and Forbid all the Peers, People and Subjects of* England, *to dare to give any*

(l) *Præcipimus & interdici- mus UNIVERSIS & ſingulis PROCERIBUS, ſubditis, popu- lis & aliis prædictis, ne ILLI, ejuſve MONITIS, MANDA- TIS, aut LEGIBUS audeant OBEDIRE. Qui ſecus fece- rint, ſimili Anathematis ſenten- tia innodamus,* Ibid. Sect. 5.

any Obedience to the Queen, her Monitions, Commands, or Laws. And if any do otherwise, we involve them in the same Sentence of Anathema and Excommunication. Whence it evidently appears, 1. That the Pope, in this Authentique Bull, and Decretory Sentence, does (so far as he is able) Depose the Queen. 2. Absolve all her Subjects from their Oath of Allegiance. 3. And (under pain of Excommunication) command and require them, (contrary to their Natural Allegiance) to give no Obedience to their undoubted Soveraign. Nor is this all; for

6. When he had done all this, he gave away the Queens Kingdom, and Dominions, to *Philip* the Second, King of *Spain*; as is notoriously known, and (m) ingeniously confess'd by (an honest Roman Catholick) Father R. *Caron*, an *Irish* Priest.

(m) *In depositione Elizabethæ Pius 5. Jus Britanniæ & Hiberniæ, ad Philippum 2. transtulit vi cujus donationis, demandatum postea Sidoniis fuit, Anno 1588, classe Hispanica instrueret. Remonstran. Hibernorum per Frat. R. Caron. Part 1. cap. 3. Sect. 4. pag. 7.*

Many more such impious Bulls there are in that Roman Bullary; in all which Kings and Princes are Anathematiz'd and deposed by the Pope, and their Subjects absolved from their Oaths of Allegiance; on pretence of that vast and extravagant Supremacy and Dominion over all the World, (which they challenge by Divine Right, though without any, and against all Reason) even over Kings and Emperors. For instance, the Excommunication and Deposition of the (n) *Emperor Henry the Fourth*, who was twice Anathematiz'd by *Gregory the Seventh*.

(n) Bullarium Romanum. Tom. 1. pag. 52, 53. Luguduni. Anno 1655. Vid. Binium Concil. Tom 7. part. 1 pag. 684.

Of

Pernicious to Protestant Princes, &c. [41]

(Of *Frederique*(*o*) the Second. By *Gregory* the Ninth, and *Innocent* the Fourth. Of our King *Henry* (*p*) the Eighth, by Pope *Paul* the Third. And (to omit all others) we have an Excommunication of all Heretical Kings and Princes, and Heretiques in general, in that famous (*q*) *Bulla Cænæ*, wherein (on *Maundy-Thursday*) an Anathema is solemnly denounced against all Heretiques, *even Emperors* (*r*) *Kings, Dukes*, and all of what dignity soever: and this Anathema is repeated every year. So that (amongst others) our Gracious King, and all his Protestant Subjects are Anathematiz'd and Curs'd once every year at *Rome*, as if their *Mons Vaticanus*, were become *Mount Ebal* (*s*) from whence all Curses were to come. Now, whether this doctrine and practices of Popes be not dangerous and pernicious to Kings, let the World Judge.

Well, but if all this will not doe; if the Testimonies of their own Writers (which both for learning and dignity in their Church, are most eminent) nor their receiv'd and establish'd Laws and Canons; nor their Authentique Papal Bulls (†) and Decretal Constitutions: I say, if all these be not evidence enough, to intitle the Church of *Rome* to this Seditious, Impious, and (to Kings, especially, if they be Protestants) Pernicious Doctrine; yet the Decrees and Canons of their own General Councils (which, (by their own Principles and Confessions) are representatives of their whole Church, and Infallible) I say, the Decrees of such Councils (if there be any such) will, and must be undeniable evidences of what I have said in this particular. And, that their approved

(*o*) Ibidem, p. 105. & p. 112. dicti Bullarii.
(*p*) Ibid. Tom. 1. p. 704. The Excommunication was dated 1535. and executed Anno 1538.

(*q*) Vid. dictum Bullarium, Tom. 1. p. 148. & Constitut. 62. Pauli 5. Ibidem, & plurias ejusdem generis Bullas ibi indicatas.
(*r*) *Etiam Imperiali Regali, Ducali, aut alia mundana excellentia fulgentibus.* They are the words of the Bull.

(*s*) Deut. 11. 29, & 27. 12.

(†) Vid. Pauli Papæ 4. Bullam 19. In Bullario Cherubini. Romæ 1638. Tom. 1. p. 602. *Qua Imperatores, Reges, &c. Hæreticos, Impertis, Regnis & Dominiis omnibus privatos pronunciat; Dominisque illa omnia esse publicanda, publicata autem sint juris & proprietatis eorum, qui ipsi primò occupaverint.*

G ved

ved General Councils have approved this Doctrine of the Popes Power to depose Kings and Emperors, and absolve their Subjects from their Oathes of Allegiance, I shall give you two or three evident Instances.

I. In the *General* (*t*) *Council* of *Lions* (for a *General Council* they do universally *acknowledge* it) Pope *Innocent* the Fourth deposed the *Emperor Frederique* the Second; That he deposed him in that Council, is undeny'd by any I have yet met with; and that it was, *after diligent diliberation had with his Brethren, and the Council* (*u*) appeares by the form of the Excommunication, registred, and upon Record *in the Body of their own Canon-Law.* Where 1. He (*x*) *deprives him of all his Honor and Imperial dignity.* 2. And then (*y*) *absolves all his Subjects from their Oathes of fidelity.* 3. And (*z*) *Excommunicates all who should acknowledge him King, or Emperor; or should Counsel, Assist, or favour him.*

II. In the *great Lateran* (*a*) *Council*, (for so they commonly call it) in which (if they misreckon not) there were no less then 1215. Fathers) it was synodically and categorically concluded, that the *Pope might depose Kings, absolve their subjects from their Oaths of Allegiance, and give away their Kingdomes.* The series and sum of the Canon is this; *First*, It is decreed, that *all Secular Powers shall expell all* (whom the *Pope and his Party* shall call) *Heretiques,*

(*t*) It is one of those General Councils, which the *Council of Constans* decreed all future Popes should Swear to maintain: Sess. 39. In formâ Professionis à Papa faciendæ, p. 250. Edit. 1514.

(*u*) *Cum fratribus nostris & sancto CONCILIO, deliberatione diligenti præhabitâ.* Cap. cum æterni. 1. Extra de Sent. & re Judic. in 6. The Title to that Chap. is............*Innocentius* 4. *in Concilio Lugdunensi.*
(*x*) *Omni honore & dignitate sententiando privamus.* Ibidem.
(*y*) *Omnes qui ei Juramento fidelitatis tenentur astricti, à Juramento hujusmodi perpetuo absolvimus*, Ibid.
(*z*) *Quoslibet, qui ei, velut Imperatori vel Regi, consilium, vel auxilium præstiterint, vel favorem, Excommunicationis sententiæ subjacere.*
(*a*) Concil. Lateranum Magnum, sub Innocentio. 3. Anno 1215. Can. 3. *De Hæreticis:* and the Canon is received into the Canon-law, by Pope *Gregory* the 9. Cap. *Excommunicamus.* 13. Extra de *Hæreticis.*

tiques, out of their Dominions, and they were to be admonish'd to do this, *Moneantur seculares potestates*, &c. Secondly, But in case they obey'd not that monition, they were to be (*b*) COMPELL'D. And not onely the *Lateran*, but the (*c*) *Trent-Council*, (a most Apocryphal Conventicle, as I shall, when required, make evident to you) useth the same Saucy Language to *Princes* and *Supreme Powers*, (*d*) (*even Emperors, Kings, Princes, and all other of what state or dignity soever*) for all these are (*e*) COMMANDED to observe all the Sacred Canons, and ALL GENERAL COUNCILS, (and so even the Lateran Council, and this Canon we are speaking of) *which are in favor of Ecclesiastical persons, and the Liberties of the Church*; and they are to observe all these, and ALL OTHER PAPAL SANCTIONS, *as the* PRECEPTS OF GOD, *and* DIVINE ORDINATIONS. And the Lemma, (*f*) or Title to that Chapter, is this.......*COGANTUR*, &c. LET ALL CATHOLIQUE PRINCES (and much more Heretical) *be* COMPELL'D *to observe* ALL *the* SANCTIONS *concerning Ecclesiastical liberty*, &c. And this is the common and usual Language of their most eminent *Writers*, of their *Popes* and *Councils*: as you may see (to omit all others) in Cardinal (*g*) *Tuschus*, the life of *Pope* (*h*) *Gregory* the Seventh by *Platina*, and in the Lateran Council under *Leo* the Tenth, where the Pope, in his Monitory against

(*b*) *Si necesse fuerit, per Censuras Ecclesiasticas COMPELLANTUR potestates seculares*, &c. Ibid. Can. 3.
(*c*) Concil. Trident. Sess. 25. De Reformat. cap. 20.

(*d*) *Imperatorem, Reges, Principes, & OMNES, cujuscunque status & dignitatis*, &c.

(*e*) *PRÆCIPIT Sacros Canones, & Concilia Generalia OMNIA, & Apostolicas Sanctiones in favorem Ecclesiasticarum personarum, tanquam DEI PRÆCEPTA, Ordinationes Dei constituta*, &c.

(*f*) *COGANTUR OMNES PRINCIPES Catholici conservare OMNIA SANCTA*, &c. In Lemmate dicto Cap. præfixo, in Edit. Concil Trident. Anno 1634. if I forget not: for I have not the Book now by me.

(*g*) Card. Tuschus, Conclusion. Pract. Juris. Tom. 6. Concluf. 41 Sect. 40, 41 61.
(*h*) *Imperator potest COGI ad Officium Execrationibus & ARMIS.* Gregorius, 7. apud Platinam, in ejus Vita.

the

(*i*) Leo 10. in Concl. Laterano, *Approbante Concilio*, apud Binium Concil. Tom. 9. p. 9. Edit. Parif. An. 1636. *RES PEREMPTORIE REQUIRIMUS.*

(*k*) *Hæretikos AB ECCLESIA NOTATOS.*

(*l*) *Si requisitus neglexerit, &r Metropolitanum & comprovinciales Episcopos Excommunicationis vinculo innodetur.* They are the words of the Canon.

(*m*) *Ut ex tunc ipse Papa VASALLOS ab ejus FIDELITATE denunciat ABSOLUTOS, & TERRAM exponat CATHOLICIS OCCUPANDAM.*

the *Gallican* Pragmatical Sanction, saucily sayes ...... (*i*) *We PEREMPTORILY COMMAND KINGS,* &c. Secondly, Well then, by this Lateran Council and Canon, we are speaking of, *Kings* are to be *COMPELL'D*, by the *Pope,* to do *their duty*; and *that is* (as the Canon tells us) *to expell all Heretiques out of their Kingdomes.* And if you ask, Who, or What *Heretiques* those are ? The same Canon tells you, That it is all those, whom the Pope and his Party, shall *be pleased to* (*k*) *call Heretiques.* Thirdly, And they (Kings and Princes) must be *COMPELL'D to take an OATH,* and *swear* they will *Expel such Heretiques*; and this Oath they must take Publickly (that all may see and know that Princes obey the Pope) for the words of the Canon are............ *Præstent JURAMENTUM PUBLICE, quod univerfos Hæreticos, AB ECCLESIA NOTATOS exterminare studeant.* Fourthly, And if any *King,* or *Prince* (*l*) neglect this duty, and (when it is *tendred*) *refuse the Oath,* or to expel Heretiques out of his Dominions; *Then the Metropolitan and the Bishops of his Province must Excommunicate him.* Fifthly, And then if he persist contumacious, and refuse to give satisfaction by expelling all Heretiques; *they must signifie it to the POPE, that he* (*m*) *may DEPOSE HIM, ABSOLVE HIS SUBJECTS FROM THEIR OATHES OF ALLEGIANCE, and GIVE HIS KINGDOME TO CATHOLIQUES.* So the Canon.

So

So that if the *Pope*, and *a Popish General Coun-cil*, very great *for* number, (but *as for Learn-ing and Loyalty little* enough) consisting of 1215. Fathers; I say, if these may be Judges, *Kings* and *Princes* are *Subjects and Slaves* to the *Pope*, who *may COMPEL them to expel* as many of *their own Subjects*, as he *shall call* (or *miscall*) *Heretiques*, out of *their Dominions*; and *impose an Oath* upon them, to *bind them to obedience*, and unless they *obey such Papal com-mands*; the Pope may *depose the Prince who disobeys, absolve his subjects from all Oathes of Allegiance*, and *his Kingdom* (*forfeited to the Pope by his disobedience*) may be *given away*, to any, *to whom the Pope shall please to give it*. Now whether *such impious* and *rebellious positions* (*approv'd* and *own'd by the Roman Church*, in her *greatest General Councils*, which, *she believes*, (at least would *have us believe*) *infallible*) be not *dangerous* and *pernicious to Princes*, and *destructive of their just rights*, let the *World Judge*. I know, that although the (*n*) *Jesuites* and *Canonists* publickly *approve* and own the *Doctrine* of this *Canon* and the *La-teran Council*, and the *consequences of it*; yet some more sober Papists do not: And there-fore two Answers (or insignificant shifts) are brought by some) to evade or mollifie, and lessen the impiety of those consequences, which are by Protestants inferr'd from it.

(*n*) See a Book lately Print-ed, call'd, *The Jesuites Loyalty*. It contains three Letters of a Jesuite (Father *Kein*, or *Keins*, (if I forget not) was the Man) in which this Lateran Canon, and all the consequences of it, are approv'd, and the Pope's Power to depose Kings, out of Popish Authors and Coun-cils) largely, and *data Opera*, proved to be *de fide*.

1. Then

	Popish Principles, &c.
3. *Answer.*	1. Then, say they, that the *Lateran Canon* is to be meant *only of Feudatary*, or *Subordinate*, not of *Absolute*, or *Supreme Princes*.
Refutation.	But this is an evident mistake of the meaning of the Lateran Canon, and *in terminis*, contradicts the express words and sense of the Canon. For,
	1. By the Canon, *All Princes*, (*Supreme and Subordinate*, and *Feudatary*) if they *refuse to expel all Heretiques* out of their *Dominions*, are to be *Excommunicated* by the *Metropolitan* and the *Bishops* of his *Province*, and then *Depos'd* by the *Pope*: but with this difference express'd in the *Canon*. When any *Subordinate Prince* was Deposed, it was with a (r) *Salvo*, or *Proviso*, for the *Rights* of his *Superior Lord*. The Inferior Lord Deposed, loses only what was his own proper *Right*; his Superior Lord loses *nothing*. If the Inferior Lord was to pay any *Rents*, or ought any *Services* to his Supreme Lord, those he did not *forfeit*; but those remain'd *due* (as before) to the Supreme Lord. But on this condition, That the *Supreme Lord* himself did not (s) *concur to hinder the expulsion of all Heretiques out of the Dominions of the Feudatary*, or *Inferior Lord*: that is, if he hindered not the Execution of the Popes commands. For if he did; then even he (the *SUPREME LORD*) must be Deposed too, as well as the Inferior Lord. The Law and Decree
(r) *Salvo Jure Dominii Principalis.* They are the words of the third Canon of the *Lateran* Council.	
(s) *Dummodo ipse (Dominus Principalis) nullum præstet obstaculum, &c.* Ibidem.	

Decree of that *Council*, involves both the Inferior and Supreme Lords, (if both be *guilty* and *negligent* in expelling Heretiques) in the same Punishments of *Deposition*, and loss of their *Dominions*. For the Canon says, ...
(*t*) That THE SAME LAW MUST BE OBSERVED CONCERNING THOSE (who have, and) *have no SUPERIOR LORDS*. That is; the *Supreme Lords*, (be it *King* or *Emperor*) if they Obey not the Pope's command, and effectually *expel* all Heretiques out of *their Dominions*; they must (by *this Canon*) be Deposed.

2. But *admit* (which is evidently *untrue*) that the Canon meant only *Feudatary* and *Inferior Princes* should be Deposed by the Pope. The *mischief* and *injustice is less*, (as a Subordinate *Prince is less than the Supreme*) but *very great:* and (even upon this *false Supposition*) this Power challenged by *the Pope*, (and approved by *the Lateran Canon* and *Council*) will be not only *dangerous*, but *pernicious* to *Subordinate* and *Feudatary Princes*. This is too plain to need any further proof.

The second Answer some bring to what we urge against *Rome* from the Lateran Canon, is this: (*u*) They deny that *Council to be a General* one, or (if it were) that *it made any Canons:* and therefore the *Doctrine* of that *Canon* (whatever it be) cannot be imputed to the *Church of Rome,* as *Approved by it*.

(*t*) *EADEM LEGE SERVATA CIRCA EOS, Qui non HABENT DOMINOS PRINCIPALES*. And this impious Doctrine was not only approved by *Honorius* 3. Pope *Innocent* 3. his next Successor, but *approv'd, confirm'd,* and referr'd into the Body of their Canon-Law by *Gregory* 9. cap. Excommuni×mus, 13. Extra, De *Hæreticis*. Afterward *Innocentius* 4. Anno 1243. *Alexander* 4. 1258. *Clemens* 4. Anno 1265. all confirm it, as appears in the *Bullarium Magnum Romanum Lugduni*, 1655. Tom. 1. pag. 109. col. 2. And least it might be thought that they have alter'd their opinion now, and are become more favourable to Princes they have lately added the confirmation of it by *Innocentius* 4. to the Body of their Canon-Law, Lugd. 1661. Vid. 7 Decret. Lib. 5. Tit. 3. De Hæret. & Schism. cap. 1. 2.

2. *Answer*.

(*u*) The Author of the Answer to the Jesuites Loyalty, London 1678. pag. 12. Father *Preston*, under the name of *Wiherington, &c.*

But

Refut.

(x) In the Bull by which *Innocent 3.* call'd the Lateran Council, the Title is this —— *Indictio sacri & OECUMENICI Concilii Lateranensis, pro. 1. die Nov 1215. In Bullario Rom. Tom. 1. pag. 87. Edit. 1655.*

But this is as *void of Ground or Truth*, as the former. For this *Lateran Council* (and the Canons of it) have been, and are universally received in the *Church of Rome*, the *Council as* (x) *Oecumenical*, and the Canons attributed to it, as Genuine, and not Supposititious, and Spurious. That this may appear, consider,

1. That *all their Writers de Conciliis* (which I have hitherto met with) do *universally* acknowledge it to have been a *General Council*, and commonly call it, *Concilium Lateranense Magnum*, and cite the Canons attributed to it, as Genuine.

2. All the Popish Writers, who have publish'd the Councils, or Epitome's, and Summes of them, (as *Crabb, Surius, Binius, Joverius, Caranza, &c.* publish it as a General Council. And *Joverius* confidently says, ... (y) *That he cannot see, with what Face any Man dare deny it to be a General Council.*

(y) *Non video qua fronte audeat quis negare hoc Concilium esse Oecumenicum.* Joverius Concil. Part. 1. pag. 110. in Lemmate Concilio præfixo.

(z) Vid. Edit. Juris Canonici Paris. 1612. & 1618. & Lugduni. 1661. &c.

3. In their last and best (z) Editions of their Canon-Law, there is (in the beginning) a distinct Catalogue of their General and Provincial Councils, acknowledged to be such, and this *Lateran* is ever reckoned amongst those which they admit as General.

4. There is a commonly received distinction amongst their Writers *de Conciliis*, wherein they (a) tell us, That *Concilia Generalia sunt.* 1. *Approbata.* 2. *Reprobata.* 3. *Partim approbata,*

(a) So *Bellarmine, Longus A Coriolano, Rives, &c.*

probata, *partim reprobata*, 4. *Nec approbata nec reprobata*, (of which last sort they make the first Council of *Pisa*. Now this *Lateran* Council, (we are speaking of) they always reckon amongst the General Councils of the first Order, or those which are approv'd by their Church. Though this distinction of Councils be ridiculous, and inconsistent with Truth, or their own Principles; as (were it my business now, or pertinent) might evidently be proved: yet (by it) it manifestly appears, that the *Lateran Council* was (in their *Opinion and Judgment*) a *General Council*; which is that for which I produce it. But further, I say,

5. In their own *Canon-Law*, (and as in others before, so in a late and *approved* (b) *Edition* of it) this *Lateran Council* under Pope *Innocent the Third*, is *acknowledged* to be a *General* or *Oecumenical Council*. For in the *Decretals*, publish'd by the Authority and Command of Pope (c) *Gregory the Ninth*, for the *common* (d) *benefit*, and with command that (e) they, (and *none else* without *Papal Authority*) should be used by all *Judges in Judicature*, and by *Readers of Law in the Universities*; and all this confirm'd by a Bull of (f) *Gregory the Thirteenth*. In the very *first Chapter* of those *Decretals*, the *Lemma*, or *Title* prefix'd to it, is thus: (g) *Innocent the Third*, *in a General Council*: And that we may be sure, 'tis the *Lateran Council* he means; a (h) great Lawyer in his Annotations, (subjoyn'd to that Bull of *Gregory the*

(b) Corpus Juris Canonici Lugduni 1661.

(c) Vide Bullam Gregorii 9. Decretalibus præfixam.

(d) *Ad communem, maxime studentium Utilitatem.* Ibidem.

(e) *Volentes ut hac TANTUM compilatione, UNIVERSI utantur, in JUDICIIS & SCHOLIS*, &c. Ibidem.

(f) Bulla hæc Romæ data Anno 1580. Jul. 1. & Corp. Juris Canon. præfixa.

(g) Cap. Firmiter 1. Extra, *De Summa Trinitate*. The Title to that Chapter is this:—— *Innocentius 3. in Concilio GENERALI.*

(h) Antonius Naldus:—— *Hoc Concilium Romæ in Laterano celebratum, Anno 1215. & Innocentii 3. 18. assistentibus Hierosol. & Constantinop. Patriarchis, & TOTIUS FERE ORBIS EPISCOPIS*, &c.

the *Ninth* before mentioned) tells us, *That this Council was held at* Rome, *in the Lateran, in the Year* 1215. *in the Eighteenth Year of* Innocent the Third. *The Patriarchs of* Jerusalem *and* Constantinople, *and the Bishops of almost the WHOLE WORLD, &c.* So that if the Title of a Decretal publish'd by *Pope Gregory the Ninth*, or the *Annotation* upon it, by *Naldus* an eminent Lawyer, and the Approbation and Confirmation of both, by Pope *Gregory the Thirteenth*, be true; it will evidently follow, that the Lateran Council was a General or Oecumenical Council: And afterwards, in the same Canon-Law and *Decretals*, we meet with this *Title* to another Chapter;..... (i) *Idem in Concilio Generali*. And it appears, (both by the former (k) *Chapters* of that *Title*; and the *Annotation* on this) that *Innocent the Third* was the *Pope*, and that *in the* (l) *Lateran* was the *Council*, which is there call'd *General*. And afterwards (m) *several times* to the very same purpose; especially in the (n) *Fifth Book* of *Gregories Decretals*, and the *Seventh Title*; where this *Impious Canon* (for *Deposing Kings, and Absolving their Subjects from their Oaths of Allegiance*) is intirely *Registred for Law*, referr'd to Pope *Innocent the Third*, in his *Lateran Council*, and that *Council* declared *Oecumenical*.

6. Lastly, To put the matter out of doubt, that the Lateran Council was Oecumenical, and made Canons, the *Council of Constans* does (o) testifie

(i) Cap. Nimis 30. Extra De Jurejurando.

(k) Cap. *Veniens* 16. attribuitur Innocentio 3. and so are all the 13 following, and this 30. of which we now speak.

(l) *Concilium Lateranum sub Innocentio* 3. so says the Annotation, ad dictum cap. 30. lit. C.

(m) Cap. Qualiter 24. Extra *De Accusationibus*.

(n) Cap. *Excommunicamus* 13. Extra *De Hæreticis*, Vid. Lemma dicti Capitis, & Annotat. lit. A.

(*o*) testifie it several times, and expresly names it amongst those General Councils, to the observation whereof the Popes were to (*p*) swear, at their coming to the Papal Dignity. And although these Authorities be abundantly sufficient to satisfie our more sober Adversaries; yet I shall add one more, which may (I hope) silence the more Confident. It is the Authority of the (*q*) Trent Council, which does expresly call it a General Council, and confirms one of its Canons.

(*o*) Concil. Constant. Sess. 19. pag. 126. Edit. in Octavo, Ann. 1, 14. & ibid. pag. 180. & pag. 312. In confirmat. Constitutionis Friderici 2.

(*p*) Concil. Co. stant. Sess. 39. in forma Professionis a Papa Electo facienda.

(*q*) Sess. 24. cap. 5. de Reformat. pag. 290. Edit. Salamant. 1588. Constitutionem, sub Innocentio 3. in CONCILIO GENERALI, quæ incipit, Quaeliter & quando, Synodus innov. t.

The sum of this Discourse is; That if the *Concurrent Testimonies*, 1. Of *their own most learned*, and (for Dignity) *most eminent Writers de Conciliis*; 2. Or *their Publishers of their Councils General and Provincial*; 3. Or many *Decrees of their Popes generally approved and received into their Canon-Law*, of the last, and (as they tell us) of the *most correct Editions*; 4. Or of their *General Councils* (for such they esteem them) of *Constance and Trent*: I say, if all these be of any validity, (and with them, some of those *Testimonies are infallible*) then it will evidently follow; 1. That this *Lateran Council* under Pope *Innocent the Third*, is (and, with them, must be) an *Oecumenical or General Council*. 2. And so, those *Impious* and *Damnable Positions* in the Third *Canon* of that Council, (1. That *Kings and Emperors may be Excommunicated by their own Bishops for not Obeying the Pope*: 2. *And Deposed by the Pope*: 3. *And their Subjects Absolved by him, from their Oaths of Allegiance*: 4. *And their Kingdoms given away*

away to those, who *Obey and please the Pope:*) I say, all those *Positions*, must be acknowledged *to be the Doctrines of the Roman Church*, being *Decrees* and *Constitutions* of her received *General Councils*, which she professeth to *be infallible*, and therefore obliging her to a *firm belief of them.* 3. This being evidently so, that the *Pope and his Party* (obliged thereunto, by their approved and *received Canon-Law*, and their *General Councils*) *do believe*, and *publickly profess*, such Impious, *Traiterous*, and *Damnable Doctrines*; it will be easie for all (who have good Eyes, and will use them) to see, how *Dangerous* and *Pernicious* such Principles are, to all (especially Protestant) Kings, Princes, and their People and Subjects. And that,

1. In point of *Conscience*, and in respect of their Souls and Salvation, if they *believe* and receive such Impious Positions and Principles.
2. In point of Civil Prudence, in respect of their Persons, Honors and Estates, if they receive them not.

1. In *point of Conscience*, if they *submit to the Pope*, and *believe* and *receive* such Heretical Positions, and Damnable Doctrines, it must of necessity, be Dangerous and Pernicious to their Souls. For this Argument will be both consequent, and evident: *To believe Heretical and Damnable Opinions and Doctrines, is Dangerous and Pernicious to the Soul*; (this all Sides confess:) *But to believe that*
the

the *Pope can Excommunicate and depose Kings*, absolve their subjects, from their Oathes of Allegiance, so as they may (†) lawfully murder and kill their Kings so Excommunicated and Deposed, is *Heretical and Damnable Doctrine*; as is declared in a great and full Parliament (*a*) on occasion of that horrid and bloody Gun-powder-Treason, in the Fifth year of King *James*) In the *Oath of Allegiance*: which Oath, not onely you and I, but all the Clergy, the Nobility, Magistrates, all Graduates in the *University*, &c. have (or should have) taken, and so (by a Solemn, and *Sacred Oath*) have *Sworn* such doctrine to *be Impious, Damnable, and Heretical*. Other Arguments I need not *use to you*, (or *any who love truth, and the Church of England*) to prove the error and impiety of such Opinions, and the danger those poor deluded Soules are in, who believe and practice them. The πρῶλον ψεῦδος, the Original Error, from which the rest follow, is that vast Supremacy, which the Pope (as *Peters* Successor (challengeth, and (when he has ability) Usurps over Kings. A power St. *Peter* never had, nor pretended to; who knew no power in himself, or any other meer Man, superior to Kings (*b*) *Submit your selves* (sayes he) *to every humane Ordinance, whether to the KING AS SUPREME*, &c. He who sayes, the *KING IS SUPREME*, does with the same breath (and undeniable consequence) say, he has no Superior. It being a manifest contradiction, to say, any thing is *SUPERIOR* to that which is *Supreme*. St. *Peter* commands all *to SUBMIT themselves* to their Kings (and there were none then but

(†) I say, Lawfully; according to their Popish Principles. 1 or 1. They say, it is not Treason to kill such a King after deposition, for he is not king then, nor his People (absolved from their Oathes of fidelity) Subjects. 2. Nor is it Murder: for their Supreme and Infallible Judge, the Pope has determin'd and made it Law, *NON SUNT HOMI-CIDÆ, qui adversus excommunicatos, ZELO MATRIS ECCLESIÆ ARMANTUR, EOSQUE TRUCIDANT.* This is the determination of Pope *Urban* the Second. And it is Law in *Gratian*, cap. Excommunicatorum 47. Caus. 23. Quæst. 5.

(*a*) *I do from my heart abjure and detest, as Impious and Heretical, that Damnable Doctrine, and Position; That Princes, that are Excommunicated or deprived by the Pope, may be Deposed or Murdered by their Subjals, or any other.* So the Oath in the Statute. 3 Jac. Cap. 4.

(*b*) 1 *Pet.* 2.13. This place troubled Pope *Innocent* the Third: and if you will consult and consider his ridiculous, as well as erroneous exposition of it; you will have reason to think him a Fool, rather than Infallible: and yet it is in their Canon-Law, Cap. Solicitæ 6. Extra. De Majoritate & Obedientia.

but Pagan and Idolatrous Princes) and obey them as SUPREME Governors; the Pope commands Subjects to disobey their Kings (if he miscall them Hereticks) to refuse any assistance or subjection to them, to take Armes against them, and tells them, that if (in zeal to the Catholick Cause) they (†) kill them (or any Heretique) it is no Murder: and threaten them with Excommunication, if they do not what he commands them. Now, let any sober person tell me, whether they can (in this case) disobey the Apostle, and obey these impious commands of the Pope, without great and apparent danger to their Soules. Our blessed Saviour (whose Vicar the Pope pretends to be) does himself pay *Tribute* (*a*) *to Cæsar* (though a Pagan and Idolater) leaving us an admirable and most pious example of that Obedience and Loyalty due, even to impious and Pagan Princes: nor is this all; for he further gives *express command*, *That all should render unto* (*b*) *CÆSAR THE THINGS WHICH ARE CÆSARS.* He acknowledgeth the Imperial Rights of *Cæsar*, of which his Impiety and *Idolatry* (*c*) *did not deprive him.* St. *Paul* (both by his *practice* and *precept*) confirmes the same doctrine.

1. He acknowledges the Emperors *power superior to his* (though he was an Apostle, (*d*) *not inferior to Peter or any Apostle,* which he twice affirms to the *Corinthians*) *I stand at Cæsars* (*e*) *Judgment Seate* (saith he) *WHERE I OUGHT TO BE JUDGED*; *if I have done any thing worthy of DEATH*: he pleaded *no exemption* from the *Jurisdiction of the Civil Magistrate,* in a *Criminal Cause* (as now every

(*f*) Popish

(*f*) *Popish Bishop does* (as by their *Law* they *may*) but he confesseth the *Superiority* of the *Civil Power*, and *Appeales* to it (*g*) *I APPEAL TO CÆSAR*, (sayes he) 'Tis evident, that all Appeales are from an Inferior, to a Superior Judge, and one who has Jurisdiction over the Appellant, and cognizance of the crime, and therefore *Paul* appealing to *Cæsar*; does (*ipso facto*) acknowledge him his legal and superior Judge. So far was St. *Paul* from believing those Popish and Rebellious Principles, and from Disloyalty, or Disobedience to that Imperial (though Pagan) Power, under which he lived; that he publickly acknowledged, and humbly submitted to it.

2. Nor was he onely in his own person obedient, and a loyal subject to the Emperor, but (Writing to the *Romans*) he did, as an Apostle of *Jesus Christ*, command them also to be Loyal and Obedient (*h*) Let every Soul (every (*i*) Man) be *subject to the higher* (the (*k*) *Supreme*) *Powers*, &c. And then he adds (*l*) *That they should render to them*, TRIBUTE, CUSTOM, FEAR, HONOR, *and* ALL THEIR DUES. By supreme (*m*) powers here, he meanes men possessing Supreme Power; and the Supreme power under which he and the *Romans* then were, was *Nero*, a *most impious Pagan*, and persecuter of *Christ* and *Christians*; and yet every soul within his Empire (even *Peter* as well as *Paul*) was (by (the *Law of God* and the *Gospel*) to be *subject to him*, to *fear*, *honor*, pay him *Tribute* and Loyally obey him. As (by the before-said Examples and precepts of St. *Paul*, and our blessed *Saviour*) evidently appears. Now your *Popish Doctrine*, and (by them

---

(*f*) Concil. Tridentinum. Sess. 24. Cap. 5. *De Reformatione*.

(*g*) Act. 25. 11. vid. R. Abbott De suprema Potestat. Regia Præfect. 6. pag. 60. 61.

(*h*) Rom. 13. 1.
(*i*) Gen. 46. 27. Levit. 12, 3. 6. 11.
(*k*) ὑπερεχούσαις, *supremæ* 1 Pet. 2. 13. It is the same word in *Peter* and *Paul* too.
(*l*) R. m. 13. 7.
(*m*) For ἐξουσίαι, Vers. 1. are ἄρχοντες, Vers. 3. and διάκονοι τȣ Θεȣ, Vers. 4.

Popish Principles, &c.

them) *Approved Principles* contradicts *all this*; and let St. *Peter, Paul* and our blessed Saviour say, or do what they will; let them *acknowledge Cæsars Supreme Power*, and *command obedience* to him (though a Pagan) and *submit to his power themselves*: yet at *Rome*, they acknowledge NO SUPREME POWER *but the* POPE; whom (as I have before (n)shew'd) they make vastly *superior, and greater then Kings*; so that (when *he thinks fit*) he may *depose a King*, or Supreme Prince, and command their subjects (upon pain of Excommunication, and an Anathema) to pay them no *Tribute, Fear*, or *Honor nor (o)* OBEY ANY OF THEIR COMMANDS: For such is the stile of their Anathema's and Damnatory Bulls, particularly of that, wherein Pope *Pius* the Fifth deposeth Q. *Elizabeth*, quoted in the Margent. This premised, as *evidently certain*; be you judge, whether it be not *a great crime* and *crying sin*, for any *subjects to believe this rebellious and Popish doctrine*, against the *express command of our blessed Saviour and his Apostles* in the Gospel? And if it be (as undeniably it is) then it is as certain, that the *beliefe and practice* of such *doctrine and principles*, is not *onely dangerous*, but (without *repentance*) *pernicious* and *damnable* to those miserably deluded Soules, who do so believe and practice it.

And it is considerable, and *undeniably certain*, that their *Popish Doctrine*, and *received principles*, do not onely *approve the Excommunication and Deposition of Kings*, the *Absolution of their Subjects* from their *Oathes of Allegiance*, their *Prohibition* of them to obey *the Lawes or Commands* of their *Princes so deposed*,

that

(n) See the place before-cited, Cap. *Solicitæ*, 6. Extra *De Major. & Obedient.* where Pope *Innocent* the Third sayes, That the *Papal Power* is greater then the *Imperial*, as much as the *Sun* is greater than the *Moon*. The Glosse there sayes; He is 47. times greater; The Note in the Margent sayes, 57. times; but, (upon mature consideration, no doubt) The Addition there, sayes the Papal Power is 7744. times greater than the Imperial.

(o) *Præcipimus universis subditis, ne illi ejusve mandatis aut legibus audeant obedire, qui secus egerint Anathematis sententia innodamus* Ita Bulla Pii 5. de Damnat. Elizab. An: 1570. Eliz. 13. In Bullario Romano. Lugd. 1655. Tom. 2. p. 303. Sometimes they are forbid in such Bulls; *Ne consilium, Juvamen Operæ, Operamve aliquatenus impendant Regi deposito.* So in the Deposition of the Emperor *Friderique* the Second. In Bullario dicto. Tom. 1. p. 106. Col. 1.

that they *may take Arms*, (and innocently *Kill all Heretiques*, (*Princes* or *People*.) But they are encouraged to do this, (by their *Popes Decretals*, approved and received (*p*) *for Law*, in the *Body of their Canon-Law*, in the last, and (as they say) the most correct Editions of that Law, approved and established by the Bull and Authority of *Gregory the Thirteenth*) with the *promise of Heaven*, *and Eternal Life*, if they die in the War against the *Enemies of the Roman Faith, Heretiques and Infidels*. This was a *fair promise*; but *Pope Innocent the Third*, (Popes having for some Ages been liberal in promising what they had no power to give) *promises more*; for besides a *Plenary Remission of Sins*, he promises, not only *Heaven*, but a (*q*) *greater degree of Glory in it*, to the *Crusado's*, the *Crucisignati*, Soldiers marked with a Cross: who (as it was pretended) were raised, to recover the Holy Land from the *Saracens*; but they, or some with the like indulgence, imploy'd to Murder the poor (*r*) *Waldenses*, which with barbarous and inhumane cruelty they did. Now how dangerous to the Soul, Sin so encourag'd must be, a weak-sighted Man may easily see, without Spectacles or further proof. Be it concluded then; such *Popish Principles* (when *believ'd and practic'd*) are not only *dangerous to the Soul*, but *pernicious*, and (without *repentance*) *destructive of Salvation*.

2. But, besides that such *Popish Doctrines* and *Principles* (in *point of Conscience*) are *dangerous to the Soul*, and (without *true repentance*) *destructive*

(*p*) Vid. Gratian. Can. omnimum 4%. Cauſ. 23. Quæſt. 5. & ibid. Can. *Omni timore* 9. Quæſt. 8. Vid. Gloſſam & Turrecrematam ad dictosCanones.

(*q*) Vid.Bullam Innocentii 3.dat. Laterani 19. Cal. Jan. Anno Pontificat. 18. & Anno Dom. 1215. Mag. Bullarii Roman. Tom. 1. pag.89. Sect.17. dictæ Bullæ. *Nos ideo* (they are the words of the Bull) *Omnibus — PLENAM peccatorum OMNIUM VENIAM indulgemus, & in retributione Juſtorum SALUTIS ÆTERNÆ POLLICEMUR AUGMENTUM.* And all this extravagant Power of pardoning all their sins, and giving higher degrees of glory in Heaven; this (as is pretended) infallible Judge, erroneouſly and ridiculouſly builds upon *the power of binding and looſing* which every Apoſtle had as well, and as much as *Peter*, and every Biſhop in the World, as much as the Pope.

(*r*) *Catholici, qui crucis aſſumpto charactere, ad Hæreticorum exterminium ſe accinxerint, illa gaudeant Indulgentia, quæ accedentibus ad Terræ Sanctæ ſubſidium conceditur.* Concil. Lateran. ſub Innocent. 3. Can. 3. Vid. dictum Leonis Papæ 4. apud Gratianum Can. *Omni timore* 9. Cauſ. 33. Quæſt. 8.

of Salvation; they are also (if consider'd *in Civil Prudence*) dangerous and *pernicious to Princes*, and *Supreme Powers*; depriving them (when put in execution) of all their *Honors, Estates,* and *Lives too.* The truth of this is (without further proof) notorious, by the sad and miserable Ruines of many great Princes, caus'd by Popes and their Party, who approved and practic'd such Rebellious Popish Principles, as we are speaking of. I say, the ruine of great Princes.

1. Before the Reformation, (who were no Protestants) and some since, who were Papists too.

2. Since the Reformation, who were indeed Protestants, or as such (or favorers of them) Excommunicated, and Deprived of their Crowns and Kingdoms; though the Excommunications did prove *bruta fulmina*, vain and ineffectual, and did not that mischief which their impious Author intended: for which we are to thank the good Providence of Heaven, and not the Pope.

1. For the first; Authentique Stories tell us, that Pope (ſ) *Zachary* Deposed *Childerick* (or *Chilperick*) King of *France*, about the middle of the Eighth Century. 2. *Gregory the Seventh* Deposeth *Henry the Fourth*, and causeth great and miserable Rebellions and Bloodshed in the Roman Empire, in the Eleventh Century. 3. Pope *Sylvester the Third,*

(ſ) And a little before him, Pope *Gregory* 2. Deposed the Emperor *Leo Isaurus*, because he was against Images, which was *Anno* 729. Vid. Baron. Annal. ad Annum 730. Num. 5. Where he has this Note concerning that Emperors Deposition: —— *Sic exemplum posteris DIGNUM reliquit Gregorius; ne in Ecclesia Christi REGNARE SINERENTUR HÆRETICI PRINCIPES.* The Cardinal every where highly approves this Doctrine, &c. Vi¹. Baron. ad Ann. 593. Num. 86.

Third, in the Twelfth Century, Excommunicates the Emperor *Henry the Fifth*, *Et Magnas turbas in Germania excitat*, (says *Vespergensis*.) 4. Pope *Innocent the Third* Excommunicates *Otto the Fourth*, in the beginning of the Thirteenth Century. 5. *Innocent the Fourth*, in the same Century, Deposed the Emperor *Frederique the Second*. In short, (to omit many others) the barbarous Murders of *Henry the Third and Fourth* of *France*, have been, and most justly were, and will be imputed to these Popish Principles, in the belief of which, those impious Assassins were confirm'd and Catechiz'd. Sure I am, that Pope *Sixtus the Fifth* did approve and highly magnifie the impious Fact of *Jaques Clement* the Dominican, who was the Murderer of *Henry the Third*, in his *famous* (and *impious*) (†) *Speech* of his, made to his Cardinals (no doubt as well pleased as the Pope) in the Consistory; and afterwards Publish'd and Printed at *Rome*: An evident Argument, that they were not (though great reason they should have been) asham'd of it: for certainly they would never have Printed what they did not approve.

(†) This Speech of *Sixtus*, was printed at *Paris*, *Ann.* 1589. according to the Latin Copy printed at *Rome*, as is attested by three Doctors of the *Sorbon*.

2. But although the Popish Positions and Principles we are speaking of, are dangerous to all Supreme Powers, (even Roman Catholiques, as appears by what is already said) yet more especially to all Protestant Princes and People: For,

1. All *Protestants* (*Kings and Subjects*) being declared *Heretiques*, are Excommunicated, and
solemnly

[60] Popish Principles, &c.

(a) The forme of that Excommunication is now extant in the Body of their Law, lib. 7. Decret. lib. 5, Tit. 3. De Hæreticis & Schism. cap. 9.

(b) The Bull of Excommunication is dated at *Rome*, An. 1558. which was 1 *Elizabethæ*.

(c) Quacunque dignitate, etiam Cœnitali, Baronali, Marchicnali, Ducali, Regia, seu Imperiali præfulgeant.

(d) Quicunque HACTENUS à fide deviarunt, seu IN POSTERUM deviabunt, seu in Hæresin incident, &c.

(e) Habita cum Card. deliberatione matura, & de eorum Consilio, & Unanimi assensu, &c.

(f) Omnes Suspensionis Excommunicationis, Interdicti, Privationis pœnas, à QUIBUSVIS, Rom. Pontificibus, aut pro TALIBUS HABITIS, per eorum literas Extravagantes, seu in Consiliis, seu Patrum Decretis & Canonibus QUOMODOLIBET contra Hæreticos Latas, approbamus, innovamus & PERPETUO OBSERVARI Volumus, &c.

(g) Regnis & Imperio PENITUS & IN TOTUM, PERPETUO sint PRIVATI, & ad illa de cætero inhabiles & INCAPACES, &c.

solemnly (*a*) *Cursed* by Pope *Paul the Fourth*, about 120 years agoe; and that we may *take notice of it*, it is *lately referr'd* into the *Body* (*b*) *of their Canon-Law*. Now this Excommunication containes many considerable particulars, As, 1. All *Heretiques, of what dignity* (c)*soever, Barons, Earls, Marquesses, Dukes, Kings*, and *Emperors* : none excepted, they are all involved in the same Curse and Anathema. 2. Nor is it onely those Heretiques who then were in being, but *ALL also, which* (*d*) *AFTERWARDS SHOULD BE*. So that our *gracious King* and his *Protestant subjects* now, are as much under the *Curse*, as Q. *Elizabeth* and her *subjects* were, in the *First of her Reign*, when that Bull *was first* publish'd. 3. Nor was this Bull *rashly made*, but *after* (*e*) *mature deliberation with the Cardinals, and by their Counsel, and unanimous consent*. It was (it seems) a premeditated and deliberate, as well as an Impious Act they were about; for impious it was and by all sober and impartial Judges, ever will be thought so. 4. The *punishments* which this Bull tyes upon Heretiques, are (*f*) *Excommunication*, *Suspension, Deprivation*, and all *other punishments*, which any *Pope*, in any *Papal Canon* or *Constitution* (howsoever made) denounced against Heretiques, all which Canons and Constitutions he approves, confirmes, and will have *PERPETUALLY observed*. 5. And for *Kings* (*g*) *and Emperors* (the same is for Barons, Earles, Marquisses,

Marquisses and Dukes) they are *TOTALLY*, and *FOR EVER DEPRIVED* of their Kingdomes and Empires, and made *incapable ever to injoy them*. The same Censure passeth upon Bishops, Archbishops, which were *Heretiques then*, when the Curse was publish'd, (*vel in posterum in Hæresin incident*) or for the future *EVER SHOULD BE Heretiques*. Nor is this Constitution (which denounceth this Curse) temporary; But, *CONSTITUTIO IN PERPETUUM VALITURA*, a Constitution and a Curse to be in force, and effectual against Heretiques, for ever. Nor is there any need, of any Legal Process to convict any person of Heresie, before the Curse come upon him: But, *EO IPSO ABSQUE ALIQUO JURIS VEL FACTI MINISTERIO* (they are the words of this impious Excommunication) All *Heretiques*, by *being so*, without *any accusation, or legal conviction*, are *actually under that curse*: So that our *gracious King*, all his *Protestant Nobility*, all *Archbishops* and *Bishops*, *Eorum etiam* (*b*) *receptatores, fautores*, &c. and all who shall receive, or any way favor them, stand *actually Excommunicated* and *Accursed*. And here I desire to know of our Papists, who do (as much as any) pretend to Loyalty; do they (as good subjects should) favor their King, or do they not? If not, then they neither are, nor can be good subjects: If they do, then they disobey their Supreme and Infallible Judges, and are (as well as we) under

(*b*) Vid. Constit. 34. Clementis Papæ 10. which next follows, & Alexan.Iri. 7. Constit. 16.dat. Romæ, Anno 1656. In Bullario Romano, Tom. 4. p. 218. where we are referr'd to many more such formes.

der the Excommunication and the Popes Curfe, and fo no members of their fo much (and with fo little reafon) magnify'd *Roman* Church.

2. But leaft this Excommunication and Curfe might not prove fo effectual as they defire, to blaft all Proteftants (which they make, for they are not fo, the worft of all Heretiques) the Curfe, to make Sure Work (as they think, and would have it) is folemnly renewed every year, in that famous (and impious) *Bulla* (*a*) *Cœnæ Domini*, read every year on *Maundy-Thurfday*. Wherein all Proteftants are (by name) curs'd, whether Princes or People. We (*b*) Excommunicate and Curfe (fayes the Pope in that Bull) *All Huffites, Wickliffifts, Lutherans, Zwinglians, Calvinifts, Hugonots,*&c. And whofoever fhall RECEIVE, DEFEND, or FAVOR them. And here again, it will concern our *Roman Catholicks* ferioufly to confider, into what ftraites, the ambition and unparalled pride of their *Popes*, has brought them. For if (according to their duty) they defend their *King*, they are curfed at *Rome*. And if they do not defend him, then they do not perform that duty of Allegiance and Fidelity to their *King*, to which (by the Law of God and Nature) they are indifpenfably bound, and and fo will be (according to their defert) accurfed in heaven. And here, It is a fhort Queftion which they are concern'd to Anfwer; Whether,

(*a*) A Form of this Bull we have in Bullar. Roman. Tom. 4. p. 528. Conftit. 34. Clement. 10. An. 1671.
(*b*) *Excommunicamus & Anathematizamus, ex parte Dei, & authoritate Petri & Pauli, ac noftra, quofcunque Huffitas, Wickliffiftas, Lutheranos, Zuinglianos, Calviniftas, Ugonottos,* &c. *Eorumque Receptatores, fautores, & defenfores.*

Whether they resolve *to obey God, or the Pope.*

3. But this is not all; for after *this Excommunication and Curse* laid upon all *Protestant Princes*, after their *deposition* and *total deprivation* of all their *royal power and dignity*, and a *perpetual incapacity brought* upon them, *disabling* them for ever to return *to those lost rights*: another *Curse* is *consequent*, and *Immediately follows* such *Excommunication*: Their subjects are declared *free from all Obligations of Loyalty and Fidelity*, due to *such Princes*, while they stand Excommunicate. This the *Decretal* of Pope (*c*) *Honorius* the Third (and 'tis *made* (*d*) *Law*, by Pope *Gregory* the Ninth, and *approved* and confirmed by Pope (*e*) Gregory *the Thirteenth*) tells us, *That while any* (*f*) *Lord remains Excommunicate, his* SUBJECTS OWE HIM NOE ALLEGIANCE *or* FIDELITY. That's the Title: and then it follows *in the Decretal,* (speaking of *a Count who* was *Excommunicate*) that the *Pope commands those to whom he writes, That they should* (*g*) *declare to the Subjects of that Excommunicated Count*, that they were FULLY ABSOLVED FROM THEIR OATH OF FIDELITY, *while their Lord continued excommunicate.* How *dangerous this doctrine* may be, to our *gracious King*, and all *Protestant Princes* (who stand actually excommunicated at *Rome*) and how *little trust* they can repose in *their Popish subjects*, I need not tell you:

(*c*) Honorius. 3. Præpositio Archidiac. & H. Canonico Suefsion.
(*d*) Cap. Grevem, 13. Extra *De Pænis*.
(*e*) In Bulla, Corp. Juris Can. præfixâ.
(*f*) Domino Excommunicato Manente, SUBDITI FIDELITATEM NON DEBENT. See the Lemma, or Title of that 13 Chapter.

(*g*) Fideles ipsas (quamdiu in Excommunicatione perstiterint) ab ejus FIDELITATIS JURAMENTO denuncietis PENITUS ABSOLUTOS. They are the words of the Law; and if you consult the Glosse and Card *Turrecremata*'s Commentary upon it, you may find more to that Purpose.

you : Seeing *such subjects*, by their authentique *lawes*, and the *declared* and *definitive sentence* of their *supreme and Infallible Judge*, are *assured* that they *owe no Allegiance* or *Fidelity*, to their *Excommunicated Soveraigns*.

4. *Nor is this all*; for there is (at least in the judgment and beliefe of our Adversaries). a far greater and more pernicious consequent and *effect* of their *Excommunication* and *Curse of Protestant Princes*. For the *mischiefs* of their *Excommunications* hitherto *mention'd*, are onely *temporal*, (though the *greatest in that kind possible*) as loss of their *Royal Power, Livelyhood*, and *Life it self*. But they say, there is an other, a Spiritual effect, which concerns the Soul, and is the greatest mischief and misery it is capable of. For they say, that *Heretiques* (*Protestants*, with them are declared such) dying *Excommunicate*, (as *all good Protestants* do) are *eternally damn'd*. For, 1. A very great (*b*) *Canonist* of our own Nation (while *Popery unhappily prevailed here*) tells us; *that every Excommunicated person is a* MEMBER OF THE DEVIL: And for further *proof of this*, he cites *Gratian*, and the (*i*) Canon-Law. And a far greater Author then *Lindewood*, or *Gratian*, and (in our days) long after them; more plainly tells us: (*a*) that Pope *Gregory the Seventh* did not onely *depose* the *Emperor* Henry the Fourth; *but Excommunicate*, and DECREE HIM TO BE ETER-

(*b*) *Excommunicatus est MEMBRUM DIABOLI.* Lindewood in Glossâ, ad Cap. *Seculi Principes.* Verbo *Reconciliationis.* De *Immunitate Ecclesiæ.*

(*i*) Gratian. Can. Omnis Christianus 32. Cauf. 11. Quæst. 3.

(*a*) *Non modo deponi, sed etiam excommunicari, & in ÆTERNO EXAMINE DAMNARI DECREVIT.* Baron. Annal. Tom. 8. ad Annum Christi 593. Num. 86.

ETERNALLY DAMN'd. And for this, he cites *Pope Gregories* own (*b*) *Epistles*, who best knew his own mind, and the *meaning of his own Decree.* So that in the Popes and Cardinals Judgment such an Excommunication is a *definitive sentence*, and a *Papal Decree*; whereby the persons Excommunicate are *consign'd and doom'd to eternal damnation.* Whence we may understand the meaning of the *Titles usually prefix'd* to such *Damnatory Bulls* of Excommunication; Such as these (*c*) ...,. *DAMNATIO & Excommunicatio* Hen. 8. by Pope *Paul* the Third (*d*) *DAMNATIO & Excommunicatio Elizabethe*, by *Pius* the Fifth, where it seems (by what the Pope and Cardinal before told us) that it is not any temporal (or not that onely) but the *eternal damnation* of Soul and Body, which is *intended* and *desired* by them, in their uncharitable and impious Anathema's and Excommunications. Whence also it manifestly follows; that all Protestants, Kings and Subjects, Princes and People) who, by many Papal Bulls and Anathema's, stand actually Cursed and Excommunicated) are in a damnable condition, and if they die (as they do, and should) without Popish absolution, by this Roman, Uncharitable, and Unchristian Divinity, they are eternally damn'd. This I say, not that I think such Papal Bulls and Excommunications either have, or can have any such effects, or bring such danger to Protestants (Kings or Subjects) as is pretended;

(*b*) Gregorius 7. lib. 4. Epist. 1. & 13. & l.b. 8. Epist. 21.

(*c*) Bullario Roman. Pauli. 3. Constit. 7. p. 704. Tom. 1.

(*d*) Constit. Pii 5. 101. Ibidem, Tom. 2. p. 303. Edit. 1655.

ed; for I believe and know, that they are *bruta fulmina*, infignificant fquibs of falfe fire; which can neither hurt their Souls here, nor hinder their Salvation hereafter. But notwithftanding this, they may prove dangerous and pernicious to Proteftant Princes, as they may be, and are great incouragements to their Popifh Subjects, to rebel, and difobey their Soveraigns, and fecurely (as to any thing of confcience or injuftice in it) act any thing to their ruine. For they who believe the Popes pretended power, that he can deprive their Prince of all Royal Power and dignity, and that he has actually done it; that he has abfolved them from all Obligations of Allegiance and Fidelity due to him; that he is a member of the Devil here, and furely to be damn'd hereafter, and that to kill him is no Murder. I fay, thofe who fubmit to the Pope, and believe thefe Erroneous and Impious Doctrines (as all muft who believe the Pope, or the Roman Church Infallible) have too much incouragement, not onely to difobey and rebel, but (when they have power and opportunity) to take away their Princes Life, as being a Perfon odious to God and Man, and by the Pope (their Infallible and Supreme Judge) by their approved Laws, and their General Councils, declared to be fuch; efpecially feeing that if they mifcarry, in that attempt (and while they feek their Princes Life, lofe their own) yet

their

their Names shall (in Red Letters) be Register'd in the Calendar, and they (by their Party) shall be reputed Martyrs; as all know, that *Campian*, *Garnet*, and our Powder-Traytors are. An honor, I am so far from envying them, that I should be very glad (and so would many thousand more) to see our present Conspirators (according to their merit) referr'd into their Calendar amongst such Martyrs; that so we might be freed from the fears of those Prodigious Villains and mischiefs they intended and indeavoured to act here, against their Gracious Soveraign, the Church and State, and there is too much reason to believe, that (while they live, and have ability and opportunity) they will prosecute those Black Designs. *Dirum omen misericors (qui solus potest) averruncet Deus.*

These are the known Positions and Doctrines of the Church of *Rome*, approved and received by the Supreme Authority of that Church; which (in *Thesi*) when they *are believ'd*, may be very dangerous, and when (in *Praxi*) put in execution (and they who believe such impious Doctrines, act accordingly) pernicious to all Kings, Princes, and People, especially Heretiques (as they miscall them) who imbrace not all their Popish Errors, in which number all Protestants (Kings and Subjects) are, by them, alwayes included. And that the *Popish Party* (*especially Jesuits*, since their unhappy appearing *in the* (a) *World*, as also their *Ecclesiastiques Secular*

(*a*) The Order of the Jesuits was approved and Instituted by Pope *Paul* the Third, Anno 1540. and highly incouraged by succeeding Popes. vide Bullarium Romanum Lugduni. 1655. Tom. 1. p. 738.

Secular and Regular (with their *adherents*) have *acted according to thofe Principles*, for *fome Ages laft paft*, and what *Barbarous Murders*, *Depofitions of Princes*, and *Fatal Tragedies*, have been the *fad confequences* of fuch *beliefe and actings*, both our own, and Forreign Hiftorians abundantly teftify. And here,

1. I fhall pafs by the horrid Murders and Maffacres of the Poor *Waldenfes*; who, (upon Profecution of the forefaid Principles) have Perfecuted with Fire and Sword, Armies (*b*) and Inquifitions; and very many thoufands (nay, *infinite numbers*) *of them*, (as fome of their own Writers teftifie) have been *inhumanely murdered*, *Caufâ indictâ & inaudita* (many times) efpecially in *France*, to fay nothing of other Countries.

(*b*) Vid. Matth. Paris ab Anno 1100, &c. *Hiftoriam Waldenfium*; *Directorium Inquifitorum, Hiftoriam Inquifitionis*, Armachanum, *De ftatu & fuccefs. Ecclef*. &c. That Directorium Inquifitorum (I mean) was Writ by Nic: Eymericus, Printed at *Venice*, 1607.

2. I defire you to *confider* that *barbarous* and *prodigious Villany*, the great *Maffacre of Proteftants in France*; *An.* 1572. where and when (above 30. or 40000. (†) *Innocent Proteftants* (in *Paris*, and other parts of *France*) were *fuddenly* and *inhumanely Murdered*, by *Papifts acting* upon fuch *Popifh Principles*, as I have before mention'd. And this Horrid Villany was fo far from being *publickly difapproved* and *damn'd* by the *Church of Rome*, or the *Impious Actors* punifh'd; that the news of it was *received at Rome* with *great Joy* (*c*) and *giving Thanks* to God for it (*Quafi author & confors*

(†) Abrege Chronlogique, &c. par le Sieur de Mezeray, Parif. 1567. Tom. 3. p. 1082, 1086. ad Annum, 1572.

(*c*) This teftify'd by Thuanus (a faithful Hiftorian) Hift. lib. 53. ad Annum 1372. p. 837. Edit. 1620. and by Fam. Strada, de Bello Belgico, lib. 7. p. 373. Editionis Romæ, 1648.

confors sceleris fuisset Deus) nor was it so at *Rome* onely, but in other places too, Papists received that news with great joy. An evident argument that they approved both that Impious Doctrine, and the pernicious effects of it.

3. To omit the many Seditions and Rebellions in the time of *Henry* the Eighth (after he had deny'd the Popes Supremacy) and *Edward* the Sixth (caused by such Persons and Principles) it is notoriously known, that the same Party, in prosecution of the same Principles and Popish Interest, did (in the Reign of Q. *Elizabeth*) *continually conspire*, and *endeavor* to take (*) away *the Life of that* good Queen, by *Poyson, Pistol,* and such other *impious* (and to persons *of such Principles, usual*) *wayes* of Assassination; to raise Rebellions and Armies (having the Popes Assistance and Blessing to incourage them to that Villany) to destroy her and her Religion. And when all this would not doe, (Heaven Blessing, what *Rome* Impiously Curs'd.) *Pope* Pius *the Fifth* (*d*) gives the *Kingdomes of* England *and* Ireland *to* Philip *the Second King of* Spain, *and he*(*with the* Popes *assistance and Blessing*) sends his (as he and his Holiness imagin'd) *invincible* Armado, to *take Possession*; But that *vast Armado*, and the *Popish Impious Design*, were utterly defeated; not so much by the Queen's Fleet (which *was very inconsiderable*) as by *great storms and tempests,*

(*) Vid. Speeds Chron. in Q. Eliz. Ann. 1584. of Dr. Parries design'd Assassination of the Queen, by the Incouragement of the Jesuits, Card. de Como, and the Pope, promising a plenary Indulgence, for that (as they call'd it) meritorious Act. See the like attempt of Ed. Squire to poyson the Queen, on the like incouragement, in *Speed* in Vita Eliz. p. 1163. num. 122.

(*d*) In *depositione Elizabethæ Angliæ Reginæ, Pius 5. Jus Britanniæ & Hiberniæ, ad Philippum 2. Hispaniæ Regem transtulit, vi cujus donationis, demandatus postea Sidonius fuit Anno 1588. Classe Hispanica instructus ut regna Britanniæ possideret.* Remonstrant. Hibernorum per fratrem. Rob. Caron. Part. 1. Cap. 3. Sect. 4. p. 7.

pests, the immediate Hand of Heaven, and a most Gracious and Miraculous Providence: And this was so evident, that the Admiral of that Armado (the Duke of *Medina Sidonia*) blasphemously swore, That he feared *Jesus Christ* was turned *Lutheran*. But *Philip* King of *Spain*, (hearing of the strange defeat and ruine of his Fleet, and seeing the Hand of Heaven in it) said more soberly, ... *That he did not send his Fleet to fight against God*, (to whose Power and Providence, he attributed the loss of it) *but against Men*.

4. The Queen being dead, *Popish Conspiracies* did not die with her; the Pope and his Party continue as industrious and (as to their Designs and Plots) as impious as before. They saw and knew, that King *James* (a Protestant) was Legal Successor and Heir to the Crown of *England*, yet used all Roman Arts, to hinder his having Possession of it; and to this end, Father *Parsons* (the Jesuite) writes a Book, to prove (what was evidently untrue, and he could not chuse but know it) That King *James* had no just Title to the Crown of *England*; (though the whole right of the *Saxons* and *Normans*, and of the Houses of *York* and *Lancaster*, were intirely and evidently united in him:) but when these Popish and *Jesuitical Arts* prevailed not, (having neither true *Reason* or *Religion* to further their *Designs*, which were *impious and irrational*),

nal) they contrive, and resolve to *execute such a Conspiracy*, as (for barbarous and *prodigious Villany*) neither *Heathens* nor *Hell* had (till that time) ever put in execution; I mean the (*a*) *Gun-Powder Treason*, which was not any ordinary or before-known *Wickedness*; (as the *Killing a King*, or *Poysoning a Prince*, &c.) but a *black and unparallell'd Villany*, worthy *Rome* and a *Jesuite*; the *Blowing up of a whole Parliament*, *King*, *Lords and Commons*, the *Murdering of a Kingdom* in its *Representatives*, and this in *a moment*, before they could see, or *dream of any danger*. But though this (for its impiety) was a *prodigious Conspiracy*, carried on with *sworn secresie*, and *lay hid*, in the *dark*, and *under ground*; yet there is no *Power* or *Policy* against *Providence*, nor *concealing any thing* from the *All-seeing Eye of our God*; He saw, and gratiously discover'd that horrid, Popish-Powder-Treason, to the *Preservation of his People*, the *Confusion of their Adversaries*, and (*nisi periisset pudor*) if they had any, to the *Eternal Shame of Papists*, and (*Popery*) their *Religion*, which approves *and encourages such abominable Impieties*.

(*1*) See the Acts of Parliament 3 Jacobi, Cap.4.5. where we are told (by the Parliament) of the *HELLISH Conspiracies of the Jesuites and Seminary Priests*. For a more particular Narrative of the horrid Powder-Plot, you may consult an ingenious Tract, call'd, *THE HISTORY OF THE GUN-POWDER TREASON*; and those Authors out of which he collected it, in the last page of that Tract; and the Authentique History of the Trial of those Traytors, now in the Press, and re-printing.

5. When King *James* slept with his Fathers, and was translated to a better Kingdom, out of the reach of such Popish Conspirators, and whither (without a serious and timely repentance of such inhumane Villanies) they can never come, their Designs slept not; they prosecure

secute their Plots and Conspiracies (to ruine our Church and establish'd Religion) as much in *Charles* the First's, as in his Fathers time. And at last it came to this issue, that (other means failing) the King (*b*) and the Archbishop of *Canterbury* must be made away. This was conceived the likeliest means to compass their Ends, and bring in that Religion *they* misc̄al *Catholique* and *Christian*. For certainly such barbarous Murders and Assassinations may possibly promote Turcism, and the Errors of *Mahomet*, (and if you will, Popery) but never were (nor can be) *any just means to propagate true Christianity*. This Traiterous Conspiracy to Murder *Charles the First*, and the Archbishop, &c. was discovered (by an honorable Person) to the English Ambassador in *Holland*, and (by him) to the Archbishop, and by him, to the King. And the Original Copy of the Discovery, being found in the Archbishop's Library, after his death, was then publish'd, and is in Print, in many hands, and (amongst others) in mine. In the mean time, our unhappy Civil Wars began; and our Popish Conspirators, (animated by a belief of such Rebellious Doctrines and Principles, as I have before mentioned, and incouraged and assisted by the Pope) are first in Arms, and the bloody Rebellion; and (in *Ireland*) murdered above 100000 Protestants in cold blood, without any provocation given, but to kill Heretiques, (which according to their impious and

---

(*b*) This Jesuitical and Popish Plot was discovered by *Andreas ab Habernfeld*, to Sir *W. Boswell* our Ambassador at the *Hague*, and by him to the Archbishop of *Canterbury*, after whose death, the Original was found in the Archbishops Library, and then printed; and is lately reprinted, under this Title, — *The Grand Designs of Papists in the Reign of* CHARLES *the First*, &c. *London* 1678. where you have an authentique discovery of that (I cannot call it worse) Jesuitical Conspiracy.

Pernicious to Protestant Princes, &c.   [65]

and erroneous Principles, was lawful and meritorious) and thereby promote the Catholique Cause. This is notoriously known to both Kingdoms, (*England* and *Ireland*.) And further, when in the process of that fatal Rebellion, (carried on openly by English, and covertly by Popish Rebels) that good King was taken, imprison'd, with design to bring his Sacred Head to the Block, (for the distance is seldom great between a Princes Prison and his Grave) our Popish Conspirators had a Council of Priests and Jesuites, which sate in *London*, and signifi'd the condition of their Affairs here, to a Council of their Confederates at *Paris*, and they transmitted the (*b*) Case to *Rome*, from whence Directions and Commands were return'd (by the *same way*) *back again* to London. In short, *it was determin'd* that it was *for the Interest of the Catholique Cause*, that the *King should die* ; and accordingly their Council of *Priests and Jesuites* in London Voted his *Death*. This is now *Notoriously known* to be true, and (in Print) *published to the* (a) *World*, by a *Reverend and Learned Person*, who (if any *shall call him to an account* for it) is so convinc'd of the truth of what he writ, that he (*in scriptis*) *publickly offers*, and promises *to make it good*. I do not hear, that he has (as yet) *been call'd to any account*, to *prove what he publickly*, and in Print, *has profess'd and promised to do :* Nor do I think, he will be call'd to any such account, because I have reason

(b) The Question put to the *Sorbon* (then almost wholly Jesuited) by our English Jesuites, sent from *London*, was (in Writing) this : —*That seeing the State of* England *was in a likely posture to change the Government, whether it was lawful for the Catholiques to work, that change, for the advancing and securing the Catholique Cause in* England, *BY MAKING A-WAY THE KING, whom there was noe hope to turn from his Heresie?* The Answer of the *Sorbon* was Affirmative. And at Rome it was resolved by the *Pope and his Council*, *That it was both LAWFUL and EXPEDIENT for the Catholiques to procure that Alteration of State, &c.* Dr. du Moulin in his Book next cited.

(a) By Dr. *du Moulin* in his Answer to *Philanax Anglicus,* (a Popish, scandalous, and lying Pamphlet) and in another Tract since ; neither of which I have here, and so cannot cite (as in Books about me I do) the particular Pages.

L

reason to believe, that he can, and will produce such Proofs, as will evidently demonstrate, both their bloody Conspiracies, and the undeniable truth of what he affirm'd.

6. By the Premises it may sufficiently appear, That the Rebellious Popish Principles and Practices have been very dangerous to all our Protestant Princes, and their Loyal Subjects, ever since the Reformation; and had they taken that effect, which they designed, and with unwearied wickedness industriously endeavoured, they would have proved destructive and (both to Prince and People pernitious. Nay, (which I have omitted) while this whole Nation continued actually in the Communion of the Church of *Rome*; when *Henry the Eighth* his Parliament and Convocation (all Roman-Catholiques, and far from being Protestants) had deny'd and (*lege* (b) *latâ*) taken away the *Popes Usurp'd Supremacy*, (that we may be sure the Pope's Practices are suitable to his pernicious Principles) Pope *Paul the Third*, *Excommunicates*, *Curses*, and (c) *Damns* the *King*, and all his *Good Subjects*; *Commands* him to (d) *Abrogate and Null the Laws* made against his Supremacy; and to appear *before him at* (e) *Rome* within Ninety Days; and his *Adherents and Favorers*, (which were all his Loyal Subjects, especially his Parliament and Convocation) within Sixty Days. They not appearing, he *Ratifies the Excommunication*, (f) *Deprives*

(b) Statut. 14 Hen. 8. cap. 12. & 25 Hen. 8. cap. 19, 20. 21.

(c) *Damnatio & Excommunicatio Hen. 8. ejusque fautorum & complicum, &c.* That's the Title prefix'd to the Bull of his Excommunication, in Bullario Romano, Lugd. 1655. Tom 1. pag. 704.

(d) *Requirimus, quatenus Hen. Rex Leges prædictas revocet, cassetʒ anullet.* Dict. Bullæ. Sect. 4.

(e) *Strictè præcipiendo mandamus, quatenus Hen. Rex per se, vel procuratorem, infra 90. dies, fautores verò, & ei adhærentes infra 60. dies compareant coram NOBIS.* Ibid. Sect. 7.

(f) *Hen. Regem privationis Regni & Dominiorum pœnas incurrisse declaramus.* Ibid.

prives him of his Kingdom and Dominions; Prohibits peremptorily the (g) King or his Adherents (if they die, as they did before he Absolved them) to have any *CHRISTIAN BURIAL*, and declares them *ETERNALLY DAMN'D*. Then he lays that most impious *Interdict* upon the whole (h) Nation; forbids all *Publick Prayers*, (i) *Masses, and Divine Offices*. Nor this only; but he *Deprives* the Children of Henry the Eighth, (k) *Born, or to be Born of Queen* Anna, and *all the Children of his Adherents*, and *their Descendents*, (none excepted) *of all their Rights, Priviledges and Goods Moveable and Immoveable*, and makes them (for the future) *incapable, and deprived* of all *Dignities, Honors, Offices, Rights, Fees, &c.* which otherwise they might have obtain'd; and this he does *knowingly*, and by the *Plenitude of his Power*. Then he goes on, and declares the King and his Adherents, and Descendents, to be *Infamous Persons, disabled to be Witness*, to *make any Will or Testament*, or to *receive any Legacy or Benefit by the Testament of any other:* (1, Forbids *all Men to have any Conversation, Commerce or Trade with them, on pain of Excommunication, and loss of all their Goods, &c.* And further, *Commands all Christian* (m) *Princes, (quacunque dignitate Imperiali aut Regali fulgeant) Kings and Emperors, no way to favour the King and his Adherents*, and (n) *Nulls all Oaths, Compacts, Treaties, &c.* (made or to be made) to or with

(g) *Si interim ab humanis decedant, Ecclesiastica debere carere sepultura, authoritate & potestatis plenitudine decernimus, eosque Anathemati, maledictioni, & DAMNATIONIS AE-TERNAE mucrone percutimus.* Ibidem.

(h) *Henrici Dominii, Civitates, &c. Interdicto supponimus,* Ibid. Sect. 8

(i) *Nequeant Missae, aut alia Divina officia celebrari.* Ibid.

(k) *Omnes Hen. Regis ex Anna, ac singulorum ejus Alharentium filios, natos & nascituros, aliosque descendentes (nemine excepto) honoribus, dignitatibus, bonis mobilibus & immobilibus, &c. privatos, & ad illa aut alia obtinenda inhabiles esse, declaramus, ac authoritate, scientia ac plenitudine similibus irrhabilitamus.* Ibid. Sect. 9.

(l) *Omnes sub Excommunicationis ac aliis pœnis monemus, ut præfatos maledictos ac privatos evitent, & quantum in eis est, ab aliis evitari faciant: nec cum præfati Regis Dominiorum, Civitatum, &c. subditis aut incolis, emendo, vendendo, &c. quamcunque mercaturam, commercium aut communionem habeant.* Ibid. Sect. 12.

(m) *Omnes Christianos Principes (etiam Imperiali aut Regali dignitate fulgentes) requirimus,* Ibid. Sect. 15.

(n) *Juramenta, confœderationes, obligationes quæ Henricum jurare possunt, irritas, cassa & inanes decernimus.* Ibidem.

the King, or in favour of him or his Adherents; and gives *Authority and express* COMMAND *to all Christian Princes, and their Armies,* (*by Sea or Land*) *to turn their Arms against the King and his Adherents, and* (a) *compel them to return to the Unity of the Church, and Obedience to the Pope.* And *whoever acknowledges* Henry the Eighth *to be King, or any way Obeys him, and will not* (*in Obedience to the Popes Command*) *expel him and them, out of the Kingdom and their Dominions ; all their Goods,* (*Moveable and Immoveable*) *Moneys, Merchandizes,* (*whether within or without* England) *are to be seiz'd on, and* (*by the Popes Authority*) *possess'd and kept by any who can catch them.* And *he there gives them* (such Thieves and Robbers) *full power to enjoy and possess such Plunder'd Goods of the Kings or his Loyal Subjects, as in their own Right and Propriety.* And *if they take any Inhabitants in* England, (*Native or Alien*) *who Obey the King, and Disobey the* Pope, *then all so taken, are to be Slaves to those who take them:* So that *Impious Bull*; in contradiction to the *Laws of Nature and Scripture, Reason and Christian Religion.* Our Blessed Saviour, (the *Prince of Peace*) came not *to destroy*, but *to save*; not to *Depose Kings* and *Emperers*, Absolve *their Subjects* from the Obligations of their Natural or *Sworn Allegiance*, or to *Arm them* against *Governors*, and (as his pretended Vicar does) *promise them a Reward* (*Remission of Sins* here, and *an higher place*

---

*rincipes & quoscunque
hates, per mare vel
quirimus, mandantes t
'en, Regem & ei ad-
dum contra sanctam fe-
;ELLIONE perman-
riu insurgant, eosque
ur, & ad obedientiam
redire cogant, eorum-
navigia, Animalia, &c.
etiam extra territo-
ici Regis) corsistentia,
NT: & sic capta in
sus convertendi, autho-
oncedimus, illaque om-
pientes PLENARIE
& personas, vel ex
o originem trahentes,
habitantes, mandatis
obtemperantes, ubi-
r capi contigerit, ca-
:ERVOS fieri deceybid. Sect. 16. 17.*

place in heaven hereafter) for *Rebellion,* and *Murdering their brethren, fellow-subjects* and *Christians,* for *believing and maintaining* that *Truth,* which by the *Pope and his Party,* should be miscall'd *Heresie.* Noe, he was the *good Shepherd,* who laid down *his own life for his Sheep* ; and when *they stray'd* and err'd from his Fold, he did not *hire and send Dogs or Wolves to worry them* ; but (with *infinite patience and mercy*) went *himself to seek them,* and *being found* (*though erring* and out *of his fold*) laid them *on his own shoulders,* and (with *great love and labor*) brought *them home* to his fold, from which (as his *sheep may,* and yet *not cease to be his sheep*) they had erred. We read indeed, that our blessed Saviour gives *Peter* commission to (*b*) FEED HIS SHEEP *and* HIS LAMBS. But we *never* read that he (*whose Kingdom was not of this World*) gave any *Commission* to *Peter,* or his pretended *Vicar,* to *raise Armies* to *kill,* and (*indictâ causâ*) to *Murder* them. Though I know there are some, who from *passe oves,* (with *bad Logique* and *worse Divinity*) conclude, that the *Pope has Power to kill Heretiques.* Like that Monk *Erasmus* mentions, who, with great zeale for the Catholique Cause, and greater ignorance, endeavoured to prove, that the Church might kill Heretiques, from that passage in the Apostle, (*c*) *HÆRETICUM DEVITA,* that is (sayes the Monke) (who had no Greek, and little Latine)

(*b*) Joh. 21.15,16.

(*c*) Tit. 3.10.

Latine) *DE VITA TOLLE*, *take him out of this life*, that is, *kill him. Sed è diverticulo in Viam.*

7. From the aforesaid reasons, I think we may (with good consequence) conclude ; *that the Pope and his party* (ever since Henry the Eighth, (*de facto*) *assum'd the Supremacy*, which (*de jure*) *was his before*) *have been in a perpetual Conspiracy against the Lives and Religion of our Protestant Princes* ; at least till the Happy Return of our Gracious Soveraign (whom God preserve) who being (by the good and Miraculous Providence of Heaven Restor'd to His Fathers Throne (His own Right and Inheritance) a blessed Peace, and all the happy effects of it, did immediately follow, to the great comfort and benefit of the whole Nation ; The Government of Church and State before shatter'd and ruin'd by a horrid Rebellion (Begun, Incourag'd, and Promoted by the Pope and his Jesuitical Party) was happily Restored, and (by Law) establish'd ; the Just Rights and Liberties of the Subjects assured to them, and confirm'd ; a Gratious Act of Oblivion, and Pardon of Illegal, Seditious and Rebellious actions against the King and His Lawes granted ; and the blessing and benefit of all these extended to *Papists* as well as others. So that besides their *Obligation to Obedience and Loyalty*, by their *Natural* or *Sworn Allegiance*, there lay upon them *an Obligation* to Gratitude,

Gratitude, for those *signal favors* they received, from the *goodness of a gratious Prince*. So that it was the *beliefe* and *hope of some*, that the forementioned *Popish Principles* and *Practises* had *been forgot*, or *laid aside*; and that the Roman Catholiques (as both in *words* and *writings* they *publickly pretended*) would be very *Loyal Subjects*. But these were vain hopes; for (notwithstanding all obligations to obedience and gratitude) even since His Majesties Happy Return, the Popish Party have carryed on their Plots and Conspiracies, against their *gratious Prince*, the *establish'd Religion*, and the *Peace of our Church and State*, with as *much industry* and *impiety*, as formerly. Which now *evidently appears*, by their *impious Conspiracy*, by the blessing of God very happily, though *lately discover'd*. That you may (in the General) know what this Plot is, and that I do not miscall it, when I say it is an Impious Conspiracy : I shall give you two Authentique Testimonies.

I. Our gratious King calls it (*a*) *A BLOODY TRAITEROUS design of POPISH Recusants, against His MAJESTIES Sacred PERSON, the GOVERNMENT, and the PROTESTANT RELIGION.*

(*a*) In His Majesties Proclamation, for banishing all Papists Ten Miles from *London*, Dated, *Octob.*30. 1678.

II. The House of Commons (in a *Vote of that* (*b*) *House*, *approved* by the Lords) say thus ......*Resolved*, &c. *That this House is of Opinion,*

(*b*) The Vote of the Commons was read to the Lords (and by them approved at a Conference, 1 *Nov.* 1678.

Opinion, that there HATH BEEN, and STILL IS, a DAMNABLE, and HELLISH PLOT, contrived and carried on by POPISH RECUSANTS, for (horresco referens) ASSASSINATING and MURDERING THE KING, and for SUBVERTING the GOVERNMENT, and rooting out, and DESTROYING the PROTESTANT RELIGION.

By what is already said (I suppose) you may see, what the Roman-Catholick, or Popish Principles and Practises have been, are, and (while there is a Pope, and a Party to believe and incourage such practises) ever will be; and how dangerous such Principles are, and when put in execution) how pernicious they are, and ever will be) to all Princes, especially Protestants, and all those they are pleas'd to call, or miscall Heretiques. Their received Principles I have hitherto mentioned are these,

1. The Pope (with them) is *Supreme MONARCH* of all the World, even in Temporals; at least *indirectè* (as the most moderate amongst them sometimes say) and *in ordine ad spiritualia*, which distinction can afford no comfort or security to Temporal Princes. For if the Pope have such vast power, *directè*, or *indirectè*, 'tis all one, he has it ; and if a Prince be deposed or murdered by *either end of the distinction*, he is equally and as

surely Murder'd; as he who is kill'd by the edge, or back of the Sword, is as certainly kill'd.

2. They say, the Pope has *power to* (*c*) *Excommunicate, Curse,* and *Damn Kings.*

3. To *depose* and *deprive them* of *all their Royal Power, and Jurisdiction.*

4. To *absolve their Subjects* from all Obligations (whether Natural, or afterwards arising from Oathes) to fidelity and obedience.

5. To *Arme their Subjects against* their *Soveraigns, soe deposed* by the Pope, their *Supreme Judge,* and (according to the profess'd Doctrine of the Jesuites, Canonists, &c.) *infallible* too, *In rebus facti & fidei.*

6. That this *taking of Armes* against *their King,* (when *deposed by the Pope*) is *noe Rebellion* against *their King*; seeing (by their Traiterous Principles) as *soon as deposed*, he *ceases* to be *their Soveraign.*

7. That, if in such a War, they *kill their King,* (especially if he be an Heretique) it is *no crime*, *noe Homicide* or *Murder,* but a Meritorious work, to which the Pope has promised *Plenary Indulgence,* and Pardon of all their sins, and an higher place in Heaven.

8. Nay

(*c*) And this vast power the Pope challenges over all Kings and Emperors, to Excommunicate and Depose them, is such; that if any King or Emperor obey not the Decree of the Pope and his Councils, he is, *ipso facto,* deprived of all his dignity, and goods, &c. It is not any private person, but a General Council of their own, which tells us so.........*Omnibus Christi fidelibus inhibet, sub pœnâ PRIVATIONIS OMNIUM DIGNITATUM & BONO- RUM Ecclesiasticorum & mundanorum, & ALIIS PÆNIS juris; etiam si REGALIS sit dignitatis, aut IMPERIALIS; quibus si contra HANC IN- HIBITIONEM fecerint, sint AUTHORITATE HUJUS DECRETI, & IPSO FACTO PRIVATI,* &c. Concil. Constantiense. Sess. 38. *In Sentent. contra Benedictum.* 13. Nay, if they be but *negligent* in executing the Decrees of the Pope and his Council, they incurre all those punishments......... *Si NEGLIGENS extiterit, cu- jusçunque dignitatis fuerit, eti- am si IMPERIALIS,* &c. *illæ pœnæ IPSO FACTO incurrat, quæ in Constitut. Bonifacii Pa- pæ 8. continentur,* cap. *Felicis* 5. Extra de Pœnis, in 6. They are the words of the same Council of Constance. Sess. 39. *In Provisione adversus Schisma futurum.*

8. Nay (to give them *the Highest incouragements* to commit *all those Villanies*, Christians are capable of) they shall be reputed Martyrs, referr'd into their Calendars in Red Letters, and (in their opinion) be esteemed great Saints in Heaven, who in Earth were known to be Rebels to their Prince, and justly Executed for High Treason. For so, as is before said and proved) those who (by the hand of Justice) perish'd for their Prodigious Villany, in the Gunpowder-Conspiracy, are reckon'd for Martyrs in the Jesuites Martyrology. Now, how dangerous such *Principles* (having such (*a*) *incouragements*) may prove to all, especially Protestant Princes, do you and the World Judge.

But (as to the danger of such Doctrines) this is not all (though too much) for it is not onely a received Doctrine in the Roman-Church, That the Pope may depose Kings and Emperors if they be Heretiques (as with them, we are sure all Protestants are) but further,

I. That Subjects also (as well as the Pope) may lawfully depose their Soveraignes, if they be Heretiques.

II. Nay, that they ought, and (both in Law and Conscience) are strictly bound to depose their Princes if they be Heretiques.

III. And their approved, and great Writers publickly confess (in their Books printed, and licensed by the Authority of their Church) that both the former propositions *are approved* by all

(*a*) Not less than 15000 Guinees promised by the Jesuites, to one who should Assassinate our Gratious King; and 4000 to Murder Justice *Godfrey*: as appears by the Papers of the discovery of the late horrid Conspiracy, and Mr. *Bedlow*'s Confession.

all Catholiques. Sure I am, they have not *publickly been condemn'd* by any Act, Decree or Sentence of their Church; and therefore we have reason to believe, that they approve them. For, *qui non prohibet peccare cum poffit, jubet.*

For the proof of all this, I shall onely give you two or three Testimonies of their own (by publick authority) approved and licenc'd Authors, who expresly say and endeavor to prove, what here I have affirm'd. 1. One of them sayes........ (b) That *it is the Opinion of ALL CATHOLIQUES, that Subjects ARE BOUND to depose an Heretical KING.* And he adds there........(c) *That they are BOUND, by the LAW of GOD, by the MOST STRICT BOND OF CONSIENCE, and UTMOST PERIL of their SOULES, to DEPOSE HERETICAL PRINCES.* And (their great Controvertist, and Cardinal) Bellarmine sayes as much; (and with more authority) speaking of Heretical Princes.....(d) *OMNIUM CONSENSU* (all Roman-Catholicks he means) *poffunt ac DEBENT privari suo Dominio.* It is the *consent* (sayes the Cardinal) *of ALL, that Heretical PRINCES may, and OUGHT to be DEPRIVED of their Dominions.* And in a Book (e) approved by the Jesuites, and highly commended by the (f) Licencer; we are told; *That the Power and Authority of the* (g) *PEOPLE is greater then that of their Prince.* 2. *That* (h) *the PEOPLE (as well as the Pope) may declare a King to be a Tyrant:* and when the Pope or PEOPLE have so declared him to be such (i) *ANY PRIVATE*

(b) *OMNIUM CATHOLICORUM sententia,* &c. Jos. Creswel, in his Philopater, Sect. 2. num. 160.

(c) *Præcepto DIVINO & gravissimo CONSCIENTIÆ VINCULO, ac EXTREMO ANIMARUM suarum PERICULO, Hæreticos Principes DETURBARE.* Ibidem, n. 162.

(d) Bellarmin. de Romax. Pontif. lib. 5. cap. 7. Sect. *Probatur.*

(e) *Mariana* de Rege & Regis Institutione Mogunt. 1605.
(f) Vid. Censuram authoritate Regia factam, Marianæ libro præfixam.
(g) Cap. 6. p. 68.
(h) Ibid. p. 59, 60.
(i) *Regem (si Tyrannus declaretur a Papa vel POPULO) QUILIBET ETIAM PRIVATUS potest JUSTE PERIMERE.* Ibidem.

VATE MAN may MURDER HIM. 3. And he there tells us, That he is a (k) Tyrant, who endeavors to ruine the Religion of his Country; (the Roman-Catholique Religion, you may be sure he means) and then (by these Jesuitical and Popish Principles) All Protestant Princes are Tyrants, and may lawfully be kill'd by any private person. So that 'tis evident, that these Popish Principles, are not onely dangerous, but pernicious to all Protestant Princes; who (in their account) being Heretiques, are consequently Tyrants, and may be declared such by the People, and Murder'd by any private man.

Object.

I know that some Roman Catholiques deny this doctrine to be approved by the Church of *Rome*, and tell us; that the Church has expresly condemn'd it as scandalous, and (both in faith and manners) erroneous: and for this they quote the (*l*) *Council of Constance*. In answer to this I shall,

1. Set down the words of the Council.
2. The Answer to them.

1. The words of the Council are these; and the Proposition they condemn this......*Quilibet Tyrannus potest ac debet licite ac meritoriè occidi, per quemlibet vassallum & subditum, etiam per insidias, vel blanditias, vel adulationes non obstante quocunque Juramento seu confederatione factis cum eo, non expectata sententia vel mandato Judicis cujuscunque.* That is ......*Any Tyrant may, and ought to be lawfully and meritoriously kill'd, by any vassal or subject of his, even by treachery or flattery; notwithstanding any oath, or confederation made to, or with him; and not having the preceding sentence or command of any Judge whomsoever.*

2. This

(k) *Tyrannus est qui SACRA PATRIA pessundat.*
Ibid. p. 60.

(l) Concil. Constantiense Sess. 15. In condemnatione illius Propositionis, Quilibet Tyrannus, &c.
Solutio.

2. This is the Propofition, which the Fathers at the (*a*) General Council at *Conftance*, condemned, (for a General approved Council, and confirm'd by a true Pope, they acknowledge it; though they have little reafon for it, as may appear by what (*b*) *Gefner* has faid, and (*c*) *Longus à Coriolano* has not (though he endeavor it) Anfwer'd.) But it is Penn'd with that Art, and Roman-Catholique cunning, that (though it feem to fay fomething for the Security of Kings and Princes; yet indeed it is (as to that purpofe) altogether infignificant. For,

(*a*) They confefs it to be *Concilium Generale approbatum, & à Gregorio Duodecimo Vero Pontifice, confirmatum*. Longus à Coriolano, in fumma Concil. pag. 858. Yet they reject what difpleafeth the Pope in it. Idem ibidem.
(*b*) Gefner in Præfat. ad Epitomen Concil. ex additis ad Chronicon Urfpergenf.
(*c*) Longus à Coriolano, pag. 865.

1. Here is nothing in this Propofition, or the Condemnation of it, by the Council; which condemns, or any way difapproves the Popes Excommunications or Depofitions of Kings, their Abfolutions of their Subjects from their Oaths of Allegiance, or giving away their Dominions. It is only the *Affaffinations and Murdering of Tyrants* which are fpoken of; not any Excommunications, Depofitions, &c. of Kings.

2. Nor does the Council deny, but that *every Tyrant MAY be kill'd*; but that which they condemn as erroneous, is; That *every Tyrant may, and alfo OUGHT to be kill'd*. Now this is a Conjunctive and Copulative Propofition; and fuch Propofitions are (in Logique) falfe, when either part is falfe, though both be not. So this Propofition, *Every Man is Rational and Learn'd*, is erroneous; becaufe one part is fo:

for

for though every Man be Ratio
Man is not Learned. In like ma
it will be granted at *Rome*, th
may be Kill'd; yet that *every*
be Kill'd, will not be so easily
let him be a Tyrant in respect
who is an Usurper, and has no
Crown; yet let him be a Rom
a Zealous Maintainer and Pr
Papal Religion and Interest;
whom they find more favour th
pect from the true King; they v
he *OUGHT to be Kill'd*. And
it was (I believe) that the
Party, did not think, *That C
(though a Tyrant) OUGHT*
or (for ought I know) ever
(though they desired and ende
away the Life of *CHARLES* i
had a most just Title to the Cr
they found more favour under
freedom from the punishments
than they ever had before; or o
the true Owner of it, possess
In *Cromwel's* time, no Oaths o
Supremacy were press'd upon
turgy and Common-Prayers we
and an *Ordinance passed*, *That n
Censured for not coming to Church*
was no way then to discover,
vict a Popish Recusant. On
the Fathers at *Constance*, migh

Propofition, (as erroneous) *Quilibet Tyrannus, &c.* Every Tyrant MAY, and OUGHT to be Kill'd; and not deny that *every Tyrant* MIGHT be Kill'd.

3. When they condemn this Propofition, (as erroneous) ..... *Every Tyrant may* LAW-FULLY, *and* MERITORIOUSLY *be Kill'd*: on the fame account the *Propofition is erroneous*, and (as fuch) might be condemned by them; and yet they might believe *it* LAWFUL to Kill any Tyrant, though not *Meritorious*.

4. When they fay, A Tyrant cannot lawfully be kill'd *per Quemcunque Vaffallum & Subditum*, by any of his *Subjects*; this is but poor comfort for Kings or Princes, and afford them no certain Security. For if a King *be Kill'd*, it is not much material, whether a Native or an Alien be the Affaffin, he is Kill'd. So that notwithftanding all the Council of *Conftance* has faid; they may hire an Alien to Kill a Proteftant Prince, as *Lopez* was to Murder Queen *Elizabeth*; and a Spaniard to Affaffinate *Maurice* of *Naffaw:* or (what was really intended and endeavoured, and probably had taken effect, had not the good Providence of Heaven miraculoufly hindred it) the Pope may give away our Nation, and fend a Spanifh Armado, (as he did in Queen *Elizabeths* time) or a French Army, to kill Prince and People, and take poffeffion of it. *Dirum omen misericors (qui folus poteft) averruncet Deus.*

5. When

5. When that Council denies this Propofition, (and condemns the Affirmative as erroneous) That *a Tyrant may be Murdered by any Vaſſal and Subject*; it is in the fingular number, (*per Vaſſallum & Subditum*) and hinders not, but that more, or the *major part* of the Subjects and Commonweal may do it: for although this Doctrine be impious and Heretical, yet (at *Rome*) it is Catholique, (or Roman-Catholique) and by many of their eminent Writers, maintain'd and juſtifi'd.

6. But Laſtly; This Sentence of their General Council of *Conſtance*, is fo far from proving that, for which it is produced; (*That the Church of Rome does not approve the Depoſitions or Aſſaſſinations of Kings*) that it evidently proves the direct contrary. That this may appear (and without any going back, or trouble) to you; I ſhall put in the (*a*) Margent, the words of the Council of *Conſtance*, (though you have them before.) Now in the words cited, it is evident; 1. That when they condemn the Killing of Tyrants, *NON EXPECTATA SENTENTIA AUT MANDATO JUDICIS*, Not expecting the ſentence or command of the Judge; there is ſome Judge whoſe ſentence and command ſhould be expected. For it were ridiculous to talk of expecting the ſentence or command of a Judge, if there were no ſuch Judge, whoſe ſentence

t Tyrannus poteſt, ac meritorie occidique Vaſſallum & am per inſidias, adulationes, non inque juramento ione factu cum eo, CTATA SENL MANDATO CUJUS CUN-l. Conſtant. ubi

could be expected. 2. Now although to us, (and in truth) Kings and Supreme Princes, neither have, nor can have any Judge: it being necessary, that the Judge be Superior in Power and Jurisdiction, to the Person Judged, (otherwise he cannot be a legal and competent Judge) and to say, That Kings and Supreme Princes have any Superior on Earth, (where they are Supreme) is a contradiction. 3. But at *Rome*, it is otherwise; the Roman-Catholiques do constantly affirm, That both the *Pope and the People*, are Superiors to Kings, and may pass sentence on them, and declare them Tyrants. 4. And therefore if Subjects may not kill Kings, (who are Tyrants) without such sentence or command, but must expect it; then if they *have expected*, and *have it*, then they *may kill them lawfully and meritoriously.* For *exceptio firmat regulam in non exceptis.* 5. And 'tis to be observed, that it is, *Sententia vel Mandato Judicis*, by the Sentence or Command of the Judge. So that if any private Person have the *Command* of the Pope or People, (who are (b) the Popish Judges in this case) or the *Sentence* of either of them, declaring any King to be a Tyrant; then this is Warrant enough (by their impious Pop'sh Politiques) for any private Person to kill such a King. From which Roman-Catholique Doctrine, it evidently follows, that when (in our late Civil Wars, and unhappy Rebellion) the Parliament had declared *CHARLES the Martyr* a Tyrant,

(b) *Regem (si Tyrannus declaretur à PAPA vel POPULO) quilibet, etiam PRIVATUS, potest JURE PERIMERE.* Mariana de Rege & Regis Institut. Mogunt. 1605. pag. 59. 60.

Tyrant, any particular Perſon (without Erecting an High Court of Juſtice, as they miſcall'd it) might lawfully have Murdered him.
6. It is to be further obſerved, that (by their Popiſh Principles) *Tyranny and Hereſie in Kings*, are *Crimes equally* deſerving *Depoſition and Death*; and every (c) Heretical *King is a Tyrant* with them. Whence it follows, 1. That if the Pope *Command* any one to kill a *Proteſtant* (or which with them is all one, an *Heretical Prince*; then (according to this Decree and Doctrine of the Council of *Conſtance*) he may lawfully do it. 2. Or if he give *no ſuch Command*, but paſs a definitive Sentence againſt any ſuch Prince, and in a Damnatory Bull declare him an Excommunicate and Depoſed Heretique; (or (d) *Favorer of them*) then any private Perſon has ſufficient Warrant and Authority to Murder him. So that when Pope *Pius the Fifth* had Excommunicated Queen *Elizabeth*, (by this their Popiſh Divinity) any one of her Subjects might (without any further Authority, or fault) have Murdered her. Now whether ſuch Principles as theſe, be not dangerous, inconſiſtent with Loyalty, and (to Proteſtant Princes) pernicious, let the World judge. Sure I am, our Kings (and Parliaments) knowing (by ſad experience) the fatal and pernicious Conſequences of ſuch Popiſh Principles, have publickly declared this their ſenſe and deteſtation of them. I ſhall give an Inſtance or two.

1. Our

(c) *Tyrannus eſt, qui SACRA PATRIA peſſundat.* Ibid. pag. 62. That is, *qui ſacra Papiſtica, & Religionem Romano-Catholicam, (quantum in ſe eſt) ſupprimit, & extirpat.*

(d) In all their Excommunications of Heretiques, the ſtile is uſually this: —— *Anathematizamus omnes Hareticos, eorum FAUTORES, & generaliter quoſlibet illorum DEFENSORES,* &c. Bulla Cœnæ, Sect. 1. In Bullario Romano, Lugd. 1673. Tom. 5. pag. 58.

1. Our Gratious King, (in a Proclamation) having spoken of the *Inteſtine Diviſions amongſt us*, it follows: ..... (e). *Which are CHIEFLY OCCASIONED by the Undermining Contrivances of POPISH RECUSANTS, whoſe Numbers and INSOLENCIES are of late GREATLY increaſed, and whoſe RESTLESS PRACTICES threaten SUBVERSION to the CHURCH and STATE.* The reſtleſs Practices are the miſchievous Conſequents of their impious Principles.

(e) Proclamation dated at *White-hall*, 16 Jan. 1673. and you have it in the *Gazette*, Numb. 853.

2. A full (f) Parliament, (and a Popiſh one too) takes notice of, and condemns the Papal Uſurpations, in taking upon them to diſpoſe of Inheritances and Kingdoms, in theſe words: ..... *The Pope, CONTRARY to the inviolable Grants of Juriſdictions BY GOD IMMEDIATELY to Emperors and Kings, hath PRESUM'D to inveſt who ſhould pleaſe him, to inherit in other Mens Kingdoms and Dominions: which we your Loyal Subjects SPIRITUAL and TEMPORAL, ABHORRE and DETEST.* Such were the Popes Uſurpations then; but (as in Parliament they confeſs) abhorred and deteſted by Clergy and Laity. But now (as evidently appears by the lately diſcovered damnable Conſpiracy) the Pope and his Party, take upon them to Murder our Gratious King, (whom God preſerve) and diſpoſe of His Kingdoms. Which Practices, and

(f) Statut. Anno 25 Hen. 8. cap. 22. which was Ann. Chriſt. 1533. and he was not Excommunicated till the year 1538. Magnum Bullarium Roman. Lugd. 1655. Tom. 1. pag. 704.

and Principles which cause and encourage them, I do (and justly may) call Dangerous, and (when they take effect, which I hope they never will) Destructive and Pernicious.

And here further, because many of our Popish Party, seeing the horridness of this Damnable and Hellish Conspiracy, and (in reality I hope, or at least) seem to condemn both it, and the Authors of it; laying the blame upon the Persons only of some few, and with great confidence, (to give it no worse name) denying the Roman Church to approve or receive any Principles, which can encourage such Conspiracies, or prove pernicious or dangerous to Princes; their Persons or Government: I shall briefly give you an account of some more of their received Doctrines and Principles, (besides those already named) which have been, and (while they are believed) ever will be prejudicial to Princes, and the Peace and Quiet of their Subjects and Dominions. For instance,

1. The Church of *Rome* expresly declares *it unlawful* for *Secular Princes* to require any *Oath of Fidelity* or Allegiance of *their Clergy*; and as expresly forbids all their Clergy to take any such Oath, if it be required.... (*g*) *Nimis de Jure DIVINO quidam LAICI Usurpare conantur, cum Viros Ecclesiasticos nihil temporale continentes, ad præstandum sibi FIDELITATIS JURAMENTUM compellunt........Sacri Authoritate Concilii PROHIBEMUS, ne tales CLE- RICI*

(*g*) Concil. Lateran. Magnum sub Innocentio 3. Can. 43. Vid. Baronium Annal. Tom. 10. ad Annum 858. Sect. 49.

RICI perſonis SECULARIBUS præſtare cogantur hujuſmodi Juramentum, &c. This is the Conſtitution of their great and Oecumenical Council under *Innocent* the Third, and is referr'd into the Body of their Canon (*h*) Law, by Pope *Gregory* the IX, and remains in the (*i*) beſt Editions of it, commended and (*k*) confirm'd by Pope *Gregory* the XIII. So that by the Popiſh Canons, and their approved and received Laws, no *Secular Prince* may require any *Oath of Allegiance* and *Fidelity*, of any of the Clergy, or Eccleſiaſtiques, nor are the Clergy to take any ſuch Oaths. And if a Clergy-man ſhould take any ſuch Oath, it is (by their Canon-Law) for ſeveral reaſons, declared *null, and not obligatory.* For, 1. They tell us, *That noe Oath which is againſt the* (*a*) *Eccleſiaſtical utility, and benefit of the Church, is valid and binding*: Nay, the Law it ſelf there ſayes; *That all ſuch Oaths againſt Eccleſiaſtical utility*, are not Oaths properly, but (*b*) *Perjuries.* And the caſe is put in their Law, *of a Prince, who fearing ſome* (*c*) CONSPIRACY *againſt him, took an Oath of ſome; that they ſhould not (for the future) be in any Conſpiracy againſt him.* They who had taken this Oath deſired to know how far they were bound by this Oath? and that Law, and *Innocent* the Third gives this Anſwer (*d*) *That they were not ſo bound by that Oath, but that they might ſtand againſt the Prince (to whom they had ſo Sworn.) in the lawful defence of*

(*h*) Cap. Nimis, 3c. Extra De Jurejurando.

(*i*) Corpus Juris Canon. Paris, 1612. & 1618. & Lugduni 1661.

(*k*) In Bulla dat. Rom. 1 Jul. 1580. Corpori Juris Canonici præfixa.

(*a*) Juramentum contra utilitatem Eccleſiaſticam præſtitum NON TENET. Lemma ad cap. Sicut. 27. Extra De Jurejurando.

(*b*) Non juramenta ſed perjuria potius dicenda, quæ contra utilitatem Eccleſiaſticam, &c. dicto cap. Sicut. 27.

(*c*) Princeps timent conſpirationes aliquas fieri contra eum, Juramentum extorſit, quod, de cætero contra ipſum non eſſent. cap. Petiiſto. 31. Extra De Jurejurando.

(*d*) Declaramus, vos Juramento hujuſmodi NON TENERI, quin pro juribus & honoribus Eccleſiæ, & veſtris, legitime defendendis, CONTRA IPSUM PRINCIPEM ſtare libere valeatis.

of the Rights and honors of the Church and their own. Now 'tis certain, that the Pope (with them) is the sole Supreme Judge in all Ecclesiastical Causes; (and such this is, concerning the Rights and Honors of the Church) and therefore if he Judge (as we are sure he will) that our Oathes of Allegiance and Supremacy, be against the Rights and Honor of that Church, of which he pretends to be the Head; neither those, nor any such Oathes will be obligatory to any of his party; at least they will think them not to be so; and so they will think, that (notwithstanding any such Oath) they may, for the benefit of the Church, and the Catholique Cause; oppose and conspire against their Prince. 2. It is a Rule in their (e) *Law* (and *in reason too*) That in *all Oathes,* it must *be understood,* that the *right of the Superior is excepted,* and must be preserved. So if a Tenent Swear Fealty to his Landlord, how great soever (so he be a subject) it must be, *salvo jure dominii principalis*; the Royal Rights of his Prince, must not, cannot be prejudiced by that Oath. This is true in *Thesi.* Now we know, that the Pope (and his party who acknowledge him) thinks that he is far superior to all Kings; and therefore if he think and declare (as we know he has done) that our Oaths of Allegiance and Supremacy are prejudicial to his rights, then neither he, nor his party will think them binding. 3. If they were confess'd to be obligatory; yet they of the

(e) *Dictum juramentum excusare non potest, in quo debet intelligi jus superioris exceptum.* Innocentius. 3. cap. Venientes. 19. extra. *De Jurejurando.*

the Popish Church, believe *he can dispense* (*f*) *with them*, and null the obligation. This is the constant Tenet of the (*g*) Canonists; who tell us; *That the Pope does usually and easily dispence with Involuntary, but not with voluntary Oaths*; yet *if he do dispence with voluntary Oaths, it is* (*h*) *valid.* Nor is it any wonder, if the Pope dispence with Oathes (voluntary or involuntary) if it be true, which *John Semeca* the Glossator there tells us..... *That the Pope can dispence against the LAW OF* (*i*) *NATURE, and against the APOSTLE.* And that we might take notice of it, those words (in the (*k*) old Editions of the Canon-Law) are put in the Margent ......*Papa contra Apostolum dispensat :* the Pope *dispences against the Apostle.* And in the latter (*l*) Editions of that Law with the Gloss (even those confirm'd by Pope *Gregory* the Thirteenth, as most Correct, and purged from Errors) they are so far from disowning that irrational and impious Gloss; that (in a Note there in the Margent) they explain and justifie it......*It is not absurd* (sayes the (*m*) Author of that Note) *for the Pope to dispence against the Apostle; as to positive Law.* So that Papists may take as many Oaths of Allegiance and Supremacy as their Prince shall please, yet the Pope (when he pleases) can dispence with them, and set them free, from all obligation of fidelity. And hence it evidently follows ; That a true Roman-Catholique (who believes this Popish Power of dispensing

(*f*) *Papa secundum plenitudinem potestatis, de jure potest supra jus dispensare.* Cap. *Proposuit.* 4. Extra. *De Concessione. Præbendæ.* vid. Spotswoods Hist. of Scotland, p. 308.

(*g*) Vid. Gratian. Can. 2, 3, 4, 5. Caus. 15. Quæst. 6. the Gloss. and Card. *Turrecremata* there.

(*h*) *Si tamen absolvat aliquem, tenet absolutio.* Gloss. ad dictum Can. 2. verbo. *Absolvimus.*

(*i*) *Dico* (sayes the Gloss) *Quod contra JUS NATURÆ LE potest dispensare et contr.: APOSTOLUM.* Glossa ibid.

(*k*) Edit. Paris. 1522.

(*l*) Edit. Paris. 1613.

(*m*) *Non est absurdum Papam dispensare contra Apostolum, quoad jus positivum.* Nota ad Glossam ad dictum Can. 2. v. rbo *Absolvimus.*

pensing with all Oaths) may take a thousand Oaths of Allegiance, and yet give no assurance of his Fidelity to his Prince; seeing the Pope may (upon their approv'd Principles). when he pleases set them free from all such Obligations. 4. But, if all these wayes, of nulling the Obligations of Oaths of Allegiance fail: yet the Popes Janisaries (the Jesuites) have a new way to prevent all such obligations of Oaths, without any dispensations; and that is by Equivocations, rectifying Intentions, and their Doctrine of Probabilities: pernicious Errors, destructive of Humane Society, and so notoriously now known to the World, that I neither shall, nor need go about to prove them, or shew the pernicious consequences of them. Sure I am, that by their Popish Principles, no Papists are (*a*) permitted to take the Oath of Allegiance to their King, or any secular Prince: and then 'tis easie to judge, what good Subjects they are like to be. For certainly, what I may lawfully do, that (on a just and serious occasion) I may Swear to do. If it be a duty, and lawful for me to obey my Princes commands, and pay him fidelity; then certainly, I may (by Oath) bind my self to the performance of it. So all men, by the Law of Nature and Moral Veracity, are bound to *speak truth*; it is both *lawful and a duty*: and therefore, when (in Judicature) I am call'd to be a Witness; I may, and (by the consent of all Nations) ought to take an Oath, to bind

(*a*) As may (to omit all others) abundantly appear by Father *Parsons* Book writ against the Oath of Allegiance: The Title of his Book is this. *A Discussion of the Answer of Dr. Will. Barlow.* And at large lately in Father *Caron's Remonstrantia Hibernorum*, &c.

bind me, and assure others, that I will speak truth. All Men (as I said, and all confess) are bound by an indispensable Law of Nature to speak truth (when there is a just occasion for it.) and yet (in Judicature) his testimony would not pass for good evidence, who (being required) would not (by Oath) confirm the truth of it. And therefore Princes have just reason to believe, that those who will not take an Oath to be Loyal Subjects, will never be so without it. And indeed the reason why Princes may justly suspect the fidelity of their Popish Clergy, who refuse the Oath of Allegiance, will farther appear, if we consider,

2. That when and where Popery prevails, all their Bishops swear absolute Allegiance and Fidelity to the Pope, and therefore cannot swear it to their Prince too. The Oath every Popish Bishop must take at his Consecration, is this ....(*b*)I. N. *from this time forward, will be FAITHFUL and OBEDIENT to my Lord the Pope and his Successors.....THE COUNSELS with which they trust me, I will not discover TO ANY MAN, to the hurt of the Pope or his Successors...I will assist them to retain and defend the Popedome, and THE* (*c*)*ROYALTIES of St. Peter, against ALL MEN ......I will carefully conserve, defend, and promote the rights, honors, priviledges, and authority of the Pope. I will not be in any Counsel, Fact, or Treaty, in which any thing prejudicial to the persons, rights, or power of the Pope is contrived: and if I shall know any such things treated of, by*

(*b*) *Ego N. ab hac hora in antea, fidelis & obediens ero...... Domino N. Papæ & suis successoribus. Consilium quod mihi credeturi sunt, ad eorum damnum NEMINI pandam. Papatum & REGALIA St. Petri adjutor eis ero ad retinendum & defendendum CONTRA OMNEM HOMINEM. Jura, honores, privilegia, & AUTHORITATEM PAPÆ......Conservare, defendere & promovere curabo. Non ero in consilio, facto vel Tractatu, in quibus contra Papam.......aliqua sinistra vel præjudicialia personarum, juris & potestatis ejus machinentur & si talia à QUIBUSCUNQUE tractari novero, impediam pro POSSE, & quanto citius potero SIGNIFICABO Domino PAPÆ......Mandata Apostolica TOTIS VIRIBUS observabo, & FACIAM AB ALIIS OBSERVARI. HÆRETICOS ET REBELLES DOMINO PAPÆ PERSEQUAR & IMPUGNABO. Vocatus ad Synodum veniam. Verba sunt dicti Juramenti. vide Pontificale Romanum, De Consecratione Electi in Episcopum, p. 57. Editum Romæ 1611.*

(*c*) Here it is *REGALIA Sancti Petri.* But this in an Addition to the Oath...

WHOMSOEVER, I *will* (*to the utmost of my power*) *hinder them, and with all possible speed signifie them to the Pope*.....*I will* (*to the UTMOST OF MY POWER*) *observe the POPES COMMANDS, and MAKE OTHERS observe them. I will impugne and PERSECUTE HERETICKS, and REBELS to my LORD THE POPE. I will come to the Synod, WHEN HE CALLS ME*, &c. This, and much more such stuffe, you have in *that Oath*. Now this is evidently an Oath of *Allegiance and Fidelity* to the *Pope*. Wherein (to omit other things) they Swear. 1. Never *to discover the Popes Counsels* (how *treasonable soever*) *TO ANY MAN* (not *the King*.) 2. To *defend the Popes ROYALTIES, against ALL MEN* (the *King not excepted*.) 3. And if any thing be treated *of prejudicial to the Pope, BY ANY WHOMSOEVER* (the *King not excepted*) they Swear (*TO THE UTMOST OF THEIR POWER*) to oppose *and hinder it*. Here is (you see) an Oath of *absolute Allegiance* to *the Pope*, without any *salvo* or reserve of *their Fidelity to their King*, which (*d*) *antiently* was in the *Oath every Bishop* took at his Consecration, as a great Lawyer tells us. And not long before him, it is certain that Bishops at their Consecration, took no Oath at all to the Pope, but onely *promised him Canonical obedience.* For in the old *Ordo* (*a*) *Romanus* (which (as all agree) was writ by (*b*) *Arnoldus Constantinensis Presbyter*, about

(*d*) Vide Hen. Bracton, De Leg bus Angliæ, lib. 2. cap. 35. Sect. 8. where he tells us, that in his time, this Clause was in the Bishops Oath to the Pope, *SALVA FIDE DOM. REGI.* Bracton flourished about the 30 year of our Hen. 3. An. Dom. 1246.
(*a*) Vid. Ordinem Romanum veterem, apud Georg. Ferrarium, De Catholicæ Ecclef. Divinis officiis. Romæ, 1591. p. 70, 71.
(*b*) So Tritthemius de Scriptoribus, &c. Possevine; Apparat. both of them, In Arnoldo Constantiensi, aud Vosius de Symbolis Cœnæ Dom. Thesi 2. p. 441.

the year 1060.) The Metropolitan (who confecrates) askes the perfon to be confecrated, thus; *Vifne Beato Petro, fuæque Ecclefiæ, ejufque VICARIO & fucceſſoribus, fidem & fubjectionem per omnia exhibere?* The Anfwer is: *Volo.* Then follows the *promife of fidelity and fubjection* to his *Metropolitan*: But with this difference. To the Pope he promifes........ *Fidem & obedientiam per omnia* (as to the *prime Patriarch.*) But to the *Metropolitan* he only *promifes* (but *fwears to neither* of them) *Fidem & obedientiam exhibere.* But to let this pafs: It is manifeft, that whenever *this Oath* to the Pope began to be exacted of Bifhops, it has been in ufe ever fince the time of Pope Gregory (*c*) the IX. who patch'd up, and (*d*) publifh'd the Decretals; In which you have the *form of the Oath* the Bifhops *then took* to the Pope; neither *fo long* by far, nor *fo bad*, as of later years has *been required of all* Bifhops; yet bad enough. For then they fwore obedience and fidelity abfolutely to the Pope (as now they do) (*e*) *CONTRA OMNES HOMINES,* (neither King nor Emperor excepted.) And we are told in fome later Editions of their Canon-law, that now, not onely all *Bifhops,* but whoever *receives any* (*f*) *dignity* of the Pope, *take an Oath,* and *fwear Allegiance to him*: and, is it poffible, that thefe perfons who do, and muft Swear fuch abfolute obedience and fidelity. to the Pope, can be faithful and loyal fubjects to their Prince? and indeed,

(*c*) Sedet Gregorius 9. An. Dom. 1226. In the year he was made Pope.
(*d*) Which was Ann. 1230. and refers that Oath to Gregory the 7th. who was made Pope, An. 1073.

(*e*) Vid. Cap. Ego. N. 4. Extra *De Jurejurando.*

(*f*) *Hodie omnes recipientes dignitatem à Papa, fubjurant.* Ita Lemma ad Cap. dictum 4. Edit. Lugduni. 1651.

indeed, are not such Popish Principles both dangerous, and especially to Protestant Princes pernicious, and inconsistent with the Loyalty of Subjects, or safety of Supreme Powers? nor is this all; there is more danger yet to Kings and Princes, from their Popish Principles. For,

3. They *Exempt* all *Ecclesiastiques* from paying any Tax or Contribution to secular *Princes*, without the Popes Leave. This is the constant Doctrine of their (*g*) *Casuists*, their (*h*) *Canon-Law*, and (*i*) *Canonists*. Who tell us (*k*) *Quod Laici Collectas imponentes Clericis, sunt excommunicati, cum suis fautoribus;* All *Laymen* (by *their Law*) are Excommunicated, if they lay any Tax upon the Clergy. And again (more fully) we are told. 1. That (*l*) the Clergy OUGHT NOT to relieve the NECESSITIES of Cities, or any other places; no, not even then when the Laicks are in want, unless the Pope be first consulted. 2. That all Decrees and Constitutions of Lay-men, laying such Taxes upon the Clergy, are null, and never can be made obligatory. 3. All persons Excommunicated for such grievances laid upon the Clergy, and their SUCCESSORS, stand Excommunicated; unless they make satisfaction within a Month. 4. And they tell us, that all this is said for a fuller declaration of the Law in this Case, that Novices may better understand it. This is their

---

(*g*) Vid. Filliucium Quæst. Moralium. Tractatu. 16. cap. 11. p. 315.
(*h*) Vid. cap. *non minus*. 4. & cap. *Adversus*. 7. extra. De Immunitate Ecclesiarum.
(*i*) Panormitan ad dicta, cap. 4. & 7.
(*k*) Lemma ad dictum, c. 4.

(*l*) *Clerici non debent necessitatibus Civitatum aut aliorum locorum, etiam ubi laicorum non suppetunt facultates, subvenire* (this is highly uncharitable) *nisi prius Rom. Pontifex consulitur.* 2. *Sententiæ & constitutiones editæ à Laicis collectantibus Ecclesiam, sunt ipso jure IRRITÆ, nec ullo tempore convalescunt.* 3. *Rectores Excommunicati ob gravamina præmissa, remanent Excommunicati, etiam post depositum officium, & successores, nisi satisfecerint intra mensem. Hæc dicit ad majorem declarationem & pro novitiis.* Lemma ad cap. *Adversus*. 7. Extra. *De Immunitate Ecclesiarum.*

their *own* Exposition of the *Canon*, in the *most* (m) *correct Body of their Canon-Law*; and they there tell us, that it is the *Canon* of a (n) *General Council*, and then (according to their Principles) infallibly true, and obligatory to all the Christian World. So that by this Popish Law, if any Lay-men (the King and Parliament of *England*) lay *any Tax*, or (by a *Statute*) require any *Subsidy of Clergymen*, (though in the *Necessities* of the Kingdom) without the Popes leave; such *Statute* is declared *Void and Null*, and *they* and their *Successors* (unless satisfaction be made) *Excommunicate*. Nor is it only some *Inferior Magistrates* or Officers, who are thus Excommunicated; but all Persons, (a) *CUJUSCUNQUE conditionis, Status aut DIGNITATIS.* And that we may know, that such Excommunications are not a rash and inconsiderate Act of *Urban the Fifth*, or some angry Pope, they have been, (for some Ages past) and still are solemnly publish'd at *Rome*, every Year, in that famous and impious *Bulla Cœnæ Domini*, on *Maundy-Thursday.* (Even on *that day*, in which our *Blessed Saviour Instituted* that *Cœna Domini*, as a Sacrament *of our Union with him*, by a lively Faith, and of the Communion *of all Christians amongst themselves*, by an unfeigned *love and charity*; I say, on this day, the greatest part of the Christian World, are Anathematiz'd and Curs'd at *Rome*, by their Popes successively, for no other reason but because

(m) Vid. Corpus Juris Canonici Lugduni. Anno 1661.

(n) Dicto Cap. Adversus 7. in Lemmate. Idem Innocentius 3. in Concil. Generali: And the Note tells us, in Concil. Lateran. cap. 46.

(a) Ita Urbanus Papa 5. Constitut. 1. Edita Anno 1364. In Bullario Rom. Tom. 1. pag. 282.

because they are *for the Truth of the Gospel*, and against his (without any reason or sense) *Usurp'd Greatness and Worldly Interest*.) In that *Bull*, the *Anathema*, or *Papal Curse* (Stilo Curiæ) is thus: (b) *We Excommunicate all, of what Dignity soever*, *REGAL, IMPERIAL, DUCAL*, &c. *who impose any Tax, Toll, or Prestation upon any Ecclesiastiques, or receive any Taxes so impos'd*, (though the Persons on whom they are imposed, *would WILLINGLY pay them*) *without the special and EXPRESS LICENCE of the Pope*. Now although this (aforesaid) were evidence enough to intitle the Church of *Rome* to such desperate Doctrine and Excommunications; yet we have further and greater evidence; I mean, their Great *Lateran* (c) *Council*, consisting of above 1200 Fathers, (such as they were) Synodically (d) ratifying the same Doctrine: and all this expresly confirmed by the (e) *Trent Council*; which tells us, That this *Immunity and Exemption of the Clergy, is, DEI ORDINATIONE & Canonicis Sanctionibus Constituta*; and therefore *Decrees and* (f) *COMMANDS*, That all the Sacred Canons, all General Councils, and all *Papal Constitutions*, in favor of Ecclesiastical Persons and the *Liberties of the Church*, be (and ought to be) *exactly observed*; and that, as (g) *THE COMMANDMENTS OF GOD*: and *admonisheth* the *EMPEROR*, *KINGS* and *PRINCES*, &c. and obliges

---

(b) *Qui Collectas, Tallias, prastationes, & alia onera personis Ecclesiasticis, & eorum, Ecclesiarum, & Benefactorum Ecclesiasticorum bonis, illorumque redditibus — absque Romani Pontificis expressa licentia imponunt; aut sic impositas, ETIAM A SPONTE DANTIBUS, recipiunt. Necnon qui per se, vel alios directe vel indirecte pradicta facere, exequi vel procurare non verentur, CUJUS CUNQUE sint praeminentia, dignitatis, &c. etiamsi IMPERIALI, REGALI, &c. prafulgeant dignitate, &c.* They are all Excommunicated every year in that *Bulla Cœnae*. Vid. *Bullam Alexandri Papae 7.* seu Constitut. ejus 16. In Bullario Rom. Tom. 5. data erat Bulla dicta, Idib. April 1656. & Bullam *Clementis Papae 10.* dat. Rom. 7. Cal. April. Anno 1671. Ejusdem Bullarii Tom. 5. Constitut. Clement. 10, 34, and in both those Bulls, Sect. 18.

(c) Concil. Lateran. sub Innocentio Papa 3. Ann. 1215. Can. 46.

(d) Concil Lateran. magnum sub Innocentio 3. Anno 1215. Can. 46.

(e) Sess. 25. cap. 20. *De Immunitate Ecclesiarum*.

(f) *Decernit de PRAECIPIT sacros Canones, & Concilia Generalia OMNIA, & APOSTOLICAS sanctiones — EXACTE ab OMNIBUS observari DEBERE*. Ibid.

(g) *Tanquam DEI PRAECEPTA*. Ibidem.

obliges them to such Observation. Nor is the *Trent Council* content with this; but (*h*) requires her Ecclesiastiques (and many more, of which anon) to (i) *PROMISE, SWEAR and VOW, firmly* (and without *all doubting*) to *believe* all the *Canons and Councils* beforementioned, (especially the *Decrees of the Trent Fathers.*) By the Premises, I think it evident; that (by the (*k*) *approved Doctrine* and Principles of the Roman Church) no *Kings, Princes or Parliaments,* nor any *LAY-MEN*, (how many or great soever) can lay any Tax upon Ecclesiastiques, (no not in the greatest Necessity, and Poverty of the *Lay-Subjects*) without express leave first had from the Pope. Now whether this Popish Doctrine, (if approved and believed) be not very dangerous and pernicious, (especially to Protestant Princes) do you judge. Nor is this all; for,

(*h*) Concil. Trident. in forma Professionis Fidei, in calce Sess. 25.

(i) *Promitto, Voveo, Juro,* Ibid.

(*k*) How dear this Doctrine of the Exemption of Ecclesiastical Persons from the Power of Laymen to Tax them, &c. is at *Rome*, appears by the *Index Expurgatorius* of Pope *Alexander* the Seventh, Edit. Romæ 1667. pag. 8. where the Command is —*Expurgædeæ sunt OMNES Propositiones contra libertatem, Immunitatem & Jurisdictionem Ecclesiasticam.*

4. Their approved and *received Popish Principles*, do not only free them, from *taking Oaths of Allegiance and Supremacy*, and *their Estates* (I speak of their Clergy) from *Taxes*, (unless the Pope consent) but their *Persons* also, (be their *Crimes never so great*) from *all Punishment* by *Kings*, or *any Lay-Court or Magistrate* of what State or Dignity soever. This is a manifest and *known Truth*, and needed no proof, were it not, that some, who have an
ungrounded

ungrounded courage to believe such *Seditious Principles,* have also (when it makes for their Interest) a confidence to deny them. But seeing some of the Popish Party do deny it, I shall endeavour to bring such Authentique and evident Proofs, as will (I hope) satisfie you, and might covince the Gainsayers (if they can and will impartially judge) of the Truth of the aforesaid Popish Position. The Proofs I mean, shall be drawn from the clear Testimonies of their own eminent and learned VVriters, their Canon-Laws, approved and received in and by their Church, their Popes Decretals, and their own General Councils. And here,

1. An eminent *Popish* (a) *Casuist* tells us, *That ALL MAGISTRATES whoever they be,* (*Kings and Princes not excepted*) *who interpose in Judicature, against Ecclesiastical Persons, in ANY CRIMINAL CAUSE, whether it be MURDER, or HIGH TREASON, are to be Excommunicated.* And this he proves out of their *Canon* (b) *Law,* and the Constitution of Pope *Innocent the Second,* in a (c) General Council, own'd and approved by them.

2. VVe have a Canon of a Council at *Paris,* referr'd into the Body of their Law, publish'd by the Authority of Pope *Gregory the Ninth,* which

(a) Excommunicantur QUI-CUNQUE Magistratus, qui contra PERSONAS ECCLE-SIASTICAS se interponunt, in QUACUNQUE causa criminali, sive HOMICIDII, sive LÆSÆ MAJESTATIS. Filliucius Moral. Quæst. Tractatu 16. cap. 11. Sect. 307. §09.

(b) Can. Si quis suadente. 29. Caus. 17. Quæst. 4.

(c) Concil. Lateran. 2. sub Innocentio 2. Can. 15.

which determines the case thus (d) *NO SE-CULAR JUDGE* may distrain or condemn *ANY CLERGY MAN,* without the *PERMISSION* of the *POPE:* and if he do, he is to be excommunicate; and to continue so, till he acknowledge and mend his fault. You see this Seditious Popish doctrine is established by the *Council of Paris,* and the *General Council* in the *Lateran*: and by 3. Popes (*Innocent* the *Second, Gregory* the *Ninth,* and (e) *Gregory the Thirteenth*) and so *must be* the doctrine of the *Roman-Church.* For it is law with them; (f) *That NO MAN must be permitted to RETRACT, or QUESTION any Papal Sentence.* And their Law says further; (g) *That ALL* the *Popes Decrees are IRREFRAGABLY* to be observed; and that so far, and undoubtedly, as if St. *Peter* had confirm'd them with his own mouth, and *Gratian* cites Pope *Agatho* for it.

3. Nay further, all *Secular Magistrates,* are (at *Rome*) every year, solemnly *Anathamatiz'd* and curs'd; (h) *who call any Ecclesiastical persons to their Tribunals, Courts, Chancellaries, Counsels, Parliaments,* &c. *or any way molest them directly or indirectly,* for it is but six or seven years since Pope *Clement* the Tenth did solemnly curse all secular *Magistrates* and *all Courts* (even *Parliaments*) who should any way *trouble the Clergy,* or *punish,* or *take any cognizance of their crimes.* So that by this Popish doctrine, our gratious King, his great Council (the Parliament) and all our Courts in *Westminster,* stand now

(d) Cap. *Nullus Judicum* 2. Extra. *De foro competenti: Judex SECULARIS, Si Clericum per se distrinxit, vel condemnet, excommunicari debet.* That's the Lemma to the Chapter in which 'tis more fully express'd.

(e) In his Bull approving and confirming the Canon-Law. Dat. Romæ. 1. Julii. 1580.

(f) *NEMINI permissum est de eo quod PAPA STATUIT JUDICARE, vel sententiam ejus retractare.* So Pope *Nicolas* tells us in *Gratian,* Can. *Nemini.* 3 Caus. 17. Quæst. 4.
(g) *Omnes sanctiones Apostolicæ sedis irrefragabiliter sunt observandæ.* That's the Lemma or Title, and the Canon follows — *Sic omnes Apostolicæ sedis sanctiones accipiendæ sunt tanquam ipsa DIVINI PETRI VOCE FIRMATÆ. Can. Sic omnes.* 2. Dist. 19.

(h) *Qui personas Ecclesiasticas ad suum Tribunal, audientiam, Cancellariam, PARLIAMENTUM, consilium,* &c. *trahunt, aut trahi faciunt directe vel indirecte carcerando, vel molestando,* &c. Vide Bullam Clementis Papæ 10, Dat. Romæ 3. April 1671. In Bullario Romano. Lugd. 1673. Tom. 5. pag. 530. Sect. 4, 15, 16.

now accurſed, and (till they become Papiſts and Slaves to the Pope, which curſed day, I hope will never come) that curſe will be continued, and every year ſolemnly and impiouſly renewed ; and I am perſwaded that a greater curſe cannot befall this Nation, than that which will procure a Popes abſolution; and free us from his Curſe.

4. In a word, the *Trent* (i) Council publickly maintains this erroneous and impious doctrine, of the exemption of their Clergy and Eccleſiaſtiques, from the Juriſdiction of all Secular powers; The *greater Crimes of the Biſhops*, (ſay the Trent-Fathers, in the *place* (a) now cited) can be examin'd and puniſhed *ONELY BY THE POPE*; and their leſſer crimes, *ONELY BY THE COUNCIL of Biſhops.* No lay-Judge or Judicature how great ſoever, (nor Kings nor Parliaments) muſt meddle with them ; they may ſecurely ſin, and need not fear any puniſhment by any Secular power. How dangerous and pernicious this muſt needs be to all Secular ſupreme Powers, let the world judge. Certainly (upon theſe Popiſh Principles) all the Clergy muſt and will much rather fear and obey the Pope who can, than their Princes, who (by their principles) have no power to puniſh them. But this is not all ; for (to omit all other) there is one pernicious Popiſh principle more, not yet mention'd, which abſolutely abrogates and deprives Princes and Kings

---

(i) *Cauſæ criminales graviores contra Epiſcopos, ab ipſo TANTUM Rom. Pontifice cognoſcantur, ac terminentur & minores, in Concilio TANTUM provinciali cognoſcantur & terminentur.* Concil. Trident. Seſſ. 24. De Reformat. cap. 5. & Seſſ. 13. De Reformat. cap. 8.

(a) And all their Eccleſiaſtiques, do promiſe, vow and alſo ſwear, that they will firmly believe and profeſs all that the Canons and Councils have declared concerning theſe exemptions— *OMNIA à Sacris Canonibus & Oecumenicis Conciliis, & Præcipue à Sancta Synodo Tridentina definita, indubitanter recipere ac profiteri ſpondeo, VOVEO, JURO.* In formâ juramenti prof. illionis fidei, in Bulla Pii Papæ 4. in calce Seſſ. 25. Concil. Tridentin.

Kings of all their Regal power, as to the Clergy. For

Lastly, It is a constantly approved and received doctrine at *Rome*, (though evidently impious and traiterous) That *the Clergy and Ecclesiastiques, are* NONE OF THE KINGS SUBJECTS, If this be *not true*, (as sure enough it is not) then their *Popish Canons* are *erroneous*, (as you shall see anon) and their *General Councils* and *Popes*, so far from being *infallible*, that they are *actually and evidently false*: For both their *Canon-law*, their *Councils*, (even *General ones*) and *their Popes* in their *Decretal Epistles* (as by the following Testimonies will appear) have *approved, received*, and by *their authority* (so far as they are able) *establish'd* and *confirm'd* this *rebellious* and *Popish principle*. But (on the other side) if they approve and acknowledge *this principle* to be true, (as constantly they do) then they approve a doctrine which is not onely dangerous, but pernicious to Princes, which dethrones and unkings them, (as to all their Clergy and Ecclesiastiques) for if they be not Subjects to any Secular Prince, then it is evident, that no such Prince can be their King; it being impossible, that any man should be King of such persons, who are none of his Subjects. And although this Popish principle be erroneous and traiterous, against the light of Nature and Scripture, Reason and Revelation; yet 'tis not all. For they do not onely say, *that the*

Popish Positions may appear to be approved by, and generally received in the Church of *Rome*; I desire you seriously to consider these following Testimonies.

1. In the Body of their Canon-Law, of their most correct (*h*)*Editions*, and (as such) publish'd by the Authority of *Gregory* the thirteenth; we finde these words (*c*) *The EMPIRE IS NOT SUPERIOR, BUT SUBJECT to the PRIEST-HOOD*. And it there follows immediately (*d*) *THE BISHOP OUGHT NOT TO BE SUBJECT, BUT SUPERIOR TO PRINCES*. And that all may take notice of this Popish Position, it is there added (*e*) *Pope Innocent the third says this, and it is FIT TO BE ALLEDG'D MUCH*. (for the Popes Supremacy he means.) And indeed Pope *Innocent* says that, and much more in that *Decretal* (*f*) *Epistle*; some of the words are in the margent. And all this, in their approved Editions of their Canon-Law (*g*) *old* and (*h*) *new*. *Panormitan* (their great Canonist) is more (*i*) express and full to our purpose. The sum of what he says (as the Author of the (*k*) *Summaries* prefix'd to that Chapter, tels *Us*) is this (*l*)
1. *The Emperor is SUBJECT to, and BOUND TO OBEY THE PRIEST.*

2. The

2. *The Clergy is* NOE WAY SUBJECT *to the* LAITY (*not to the King*) *but onely for some Lay-Fee, or Farme held of him.* 3. *The* CLERGY BY THE LAW OF GOD, *are* EXEMPT *from the* JURISDICTION *of* LAYMEN. And no wonder, if the IMPERIAL POWER muſt be *ſubject* to the PONTIFICAL; if it be true, which their *Canon-Law* (*a*) (out of the Decretal of *Pope Innocent the Third*) the Author of the (*b*) *Gloſſe*, and the (*c*) Additions to it, ſay. For the Pope in that *Law*, ſayes; *That the Popes power, is as much greater than the Emperors, as* THE SUN *is greater than the* MOON. 2. The *Gloſs* ſayes (for ſo, in his Arithmatique, the *difference* is *ignorantly* and *wildly* computed) that the *Popes power* is. 47. times *greater than the Emperors*: and *the Addition* to the *Gloſs* (in their beſt Editions of the (*d*) Canon-Law) further tells us (out of *Ptolemy*) that the Sun is greater than the Moon. 7744. times; and ſo (by this their Account) the *Pontifical power*, is no leſs than 7744 times *greater than the Imperial*; and then there is no doubt, but in their Opinion who believe all this, the Emperor and all Kings muſt be the Popes Subjects, and they no way ſuperior to him.

(*a*) Cap. Solicitæ 5. Extra De Majorit. et obedientia.

(*b*) Bernard. de Botano Canonicus Bononienſis in Gloſſa, ad verbum, Inter ſolem. Ib.
(*c*) Laurentius in his Addition to the Gloſſe.

(*d*) Vide Corpus Juris Canonici, cum Gloſſis. Paris. 1612

2. Pope *Martin the Fifth* cites the Decretal of *Pope Innocent the Third*, and more fully explains the meaning of it, approves (*e*) and confirms it, and both their Decretals are now referr'd into the body of their Law (where

(*e*) Cap. Ad reprimendæ. 3. De Foro competenti. In. 7. Edit. Juris Canonici, Lug. l. 1661.

Pope

(f) *Laicis in Clericos NULLA POTESTAS* &c. Lemma ad dictum Caput.
(g) *Non attendentes, quod LAICIS in CLERICOS, ECCLESIASTICAS personas, aut EORUM BONA, NULLA sit attributa POTESTAS*, Ibid. Ca pite dicto.
(h) Cap. Quia. 2. De foro competenti. in 7.

(i) *Cujuscunque præminentiæ, dignitatis, status, aut conditionis existant.* Ibidem:
(k) *Principes, marchiones, Duces.* &c. *non possunt sine culpâ. SACRILEGII, Clericos bannire aut relegare..* Ibidim.

(l) *Persona CUJUSLIBET CLERICI est SANCTA quoad hoc, quod NON POTEST SUBJICI POTESTATI SECULARI, & is qui contrarium facit, SACRILEGUS est.* Cajetan. in Aquinat. 2. 2. Quæst. 99. Art. 3. Sect. ad. 5. dubium. And much more to the same purpose, we have in those 2 Titles. 1. De foro competenti; and 2. De Invasoribus bonorum Ecclesiæ in 7. Decretalium.
(m) 1. *Reges non habent potestatem coactivam in Ecclesiasticos.* 2. *Ecclesiastici non possunt conveniri, nisi coram superiori suo Ecclesiastico.* 3. *EXEMPTIO CLERICORUM, est ex OMNIUM SENTENTIA, de Jure DIVINO, ita ut à potestatibus secularibus, ETIAM SUPREMIS, judicari aut condemnari nequeant.* Vid. Collegii Bononiensis Responsum pro libertate Eccles. Bonon. 1607. Sect. 11. 46, &c.

Pope Martins *Decretal* was not before:) The Lemma, or *Title* to the Chapter before cited, is this (f) ....*Lay-men have NOE POWER OVER CLERGY-MEN*, &c. And the Decretal it self sayes (g) ....*That LAY-MEM have NOE AUTHORITY over the Clergy, ECCLESIASTICAL PERSONS, or their GOODS.* Pope *Urban the Sixth* has the *very same* (h) *words, approves,* and (by his Papal Authority) confirmes them; and declares *all Lay-men* (of (i) *what eminence soever*) who exercise *any jurisdiction* over *Ecclesiastiques*, (k) *Sacrilegious*, and *Excommunicates* them, and all whoever assist, abett, or defend them.

3. Cardinal *Cajetan*, who (his great learning, and eminent place in Government of that Church considered) could *not be ignorant* what *Positions were Approved* at *Rome*; tells us (l) ....*That the Person of EVERY CLERGY-MAN, was SACRED thus far, that he COULD NOT BE SUBJECT to any SECULAR POWER.*

4. Nay, a whole Learned Colledge assures us, of the truth of the 3 Propositions. 1. *KINGS* (m) *have NO COACTIVE POWER over ECCLESIASTIQUES.* 2. *ECCLESIASTIQUES cannot be sued, or call'd to an account, before any, save onely THEIR ECCLESIASTICAL Superior.* 3. *The EXEMPTION of the Clergy, is IN THE JUDGMENT OF ALL* (all Papists

Papists they mean) *of DIVINE RIGHT; so that they cannot be JUDG'D, or PUNISH'D by any SECULAR, no NOT SUPREME POWERS.* And here I desire you to consider ; (what the Colledge of *Bononia* here affirms) that the Ecclesiastiques (Secular and Regular) are, in the Opinion of *ALL ROMAN-CATHOLIQUES, by the LAW OF GOD,* so (†) exempted from the Jurisdiction of all Secular, (even *SUPREME*) *POWERS,* that they can neither *Judge,* nor *punish* them. Whence it evidently follows, 1. That the *Popish Clergy,* where ever they are (especially in *England,* and *Protestant* Kingdoms) are *no Subjects of that King,* in whose *dominions they live,* because they are (*by the Law of God*) exempt from *all Secular Jurisdiction :* It being a contradiction to say, that any Man is a King in respect of those, over whom he has no Jurisdiction. And, 2. It follows ; that this *impious and traiterous Doctrine* and *Position,* is not the *opinion of some one,* or a *few private persons,* but of *ALL ROMAN-CATHOLIQUES* ; and so of their Popish Church ; and then their Church (by their own Confession) *is guilty* of maintaining and approving such *dangerous,* and to *all* (especially *Protestant*) *Kings,* Pernicious Principles. Q. E. D.

(†) Vid. cap. *Et quid.* 4. extra. De foro competenti, in 7. where the Title, or Lemma is this......*Constitutiones editæ contra Principes Seculares, Jurisdictionis Ecclesiasticæ liberatem impedientes, Innovantur.* And in the Chapter, it is declared, 1. *Quod Laicis in Clericos, & personas Ecclesiasticas, & bona Ecclesiastica; non est attributa potestas,* 2. And then it follows......*REGES, DUCES, MARCHIONES,* &c. in virtute Sanctæ OBE-DIENTIÆ MANDANTES, *ut ipsi constitutiones prædictas observent.......Si Dei offensam, & SEDIS APOSTOLICÆ vitare voluerint ULTIONEM.* Kings cannot meddle with any Ecclesiastical persons ; if they do, they offend God, and shall be punish'd by the Pope: that is, Excommunicated. So sayes the Pope, and his Lateran Council Cap. 2. *De Invasor. & Occup. Bon. Ecclesiæ.* in 7. Decretalium.

5. But we have greater Authority (then that of the Colledge of *Bononia*) to manifest the truth of what we say, when we accuse the Popish

pish Church for approving and maintaining this impious and pernicious doctrine ; *That their Ecclesiastiques are not the Kings Subjects.* I mean the Inquisitors of (*a*) *Spain* and (*b*) *Portugal,* &c. who finding in the Index of *Chrysostome,* (*c.*) words expressing this proposition (*d.*) *PRIESTS, BY THE LAW OF GOD, ARE SUBJECT TO PRINCES* ; they (knowing that *Position* to be *inconsistent* with the *Exemptions* of their Popish Clergy) *damne* that Proposition, and command it to be blotted out: *Deleantur illa verba* (say they) though *Chrysostome* say the very *same thing,* in the *place to which the Index refers.* Now it is evident, that they who damn this Proposition (as erroneous) *PRIESTS by the Law of God, are subject to Princes;* must (of necessity) approve and affirm the contradictory ; *That Priests, by the Law of God ARE NOT subject to Princes* : which is that Rebellious Position, with which the Church of *Rome* is justly charg'd.

(*a*) Index Expurgatorius Hispanicus Madriti, Anno 1667 in Iohanne Chrysost. pag. 703.
(*b*) Index Expurg. Lusitan. Olysip. 1624. pag. 753.
(*c*) Edit. Basil. 1569.
(*d*) *Sacerdotes etiam Principibus Jure Divino subditi.*

6. *Lastly;* the principal Authorities I have brought to prove this (or any of the former Rebellious Doctrines charg'd on the Church of *Rome*) have been, 1. Their *approved*, and (by *Publick Authority* of *their Church*) received and *establish'd Lawes*; 2. Their *Popes Bulls, Decretalls* and *Constitutions.* 3. Or the *Canons of their Provincial, National,* or *General Councils:* All which are *approved, innovated* and *confirm'd* expresly, in their Trent (*e*) Council

(*e*) Consil. Trident. sess. 25 De Reformat. Cap. 20. *Præcipit sancta Synodus, Sacros CANONES, et Consilia Generalia OMNIA, nec non alias APOSTOLICAS SANCTIONES, in favorem Ecclesiasticarum personarum, & libertatis Ecclesiasticæ, & contra ejus Violatores editos, quæ OMNIA præsenti Decreto INNOVAT, EXACTE ab OMNIBUS observari debere.*

cil, (as was before mentioned) and all their (*f*) *Secular Clergy,* all who have *any cure of Soules,* the chief of their *Regulars,* (*g*) *all Graduates, Professors and Readers in their Universities,* (*h*) all *Physitians,* &c. are *solemnly* (*i*) *sworn to approve, receive, and (without all doubting) to profess all those Canons and Papal Constitutions, and, to Anathematize, Reject, and Curse all contrary Opinions, and to endeavour (as much as in them lies) that all committed to their care, shall constantly hold and teach the same.*

The Premises impartially consider'd, I think two things may, and will evidently follow;

1. That the *Principles and Positions* before mention'd, are not onely *dangerous,* but *pernicious* to all *Supreme Powers*; (especially to *Protestant Kings and Princes*) and that in one thing omitted before; that is; That *Faith is not to be kept with Heretiques,*.but that any competent *Ecclesiastical Judge,* may *condemn,* and *execute Heretiques,* (or those who are *reputed* such) notwithstanding *any SAFE CONDUCT given them,* BY THE EMPEROR, KINGS, or SECULAR PRINCES, *though confirm'd by OATH*; and this impious, and (to Supreme Powers) *pernicious Doctrine, approved,* and *publickly declared* and *profess'd*; not onely by particular, and *private persons,* but by their *own General* (*k*) *Council of Constance:* which *condemn'd.* (*l*) and executed *Jerome of Prague,*

and

(*f*) Vide Bullam Pii 4. super forma juramenti Professionis fidei, in calce Sess. 25. Concilii Trident. datam Romæ.Id. Nov. 1564.
(*g*) Vid. Bullam Pii 4. Extra *De Magistris & Doctoribus* cap. In *sacrosancta.* 2. In Septimo.
(*h*) Vid. Bullam Pii Papæ 5. Extra *De Medicis,* cap. supra gregem. 1. Decret. 7.
(*i*) Vide dictam Pii 4. Bullam, super forma Juramenti Profess. fidei, & Concil Trident. Sess. 24. De Reformat. cap. 12. Item *OMNIA à sacris Canonibus, & Oecumenicis Conciliis, ac præcipue à Sacrosanctæ Synodo Tridentdefinita,iNDUBITANTER recipio ac profiteor, ac CONTRARIA OMNIA rejicio ac Anathematizo, ac a meis subditis, vel illis, quorum cura ad me spectat, teneri, doceri, & prædicari (quantum in me est) curabo.* Verba sunt dictæ Bullæ Pii Papæ 4.

(*k*) *Quod non obstantibus salvis Conductibus IMPERATORIS, REGUM, & SECULI PRINCIPUM, QUOCUNQUE VINCULO SE OBSTRINXERINT,possit per Judicem competentem, de Hæretica pravitate inquiri.&c.* Concil. Constantiense. Sess. 19.
(*l*) Consil. Constant. Sess. 21. damnatio Hieronymi Pragensis Sess. 45. damnatio Johan. Hus.

John Hus, notwithstanding the Emperors Safe Conduct, without which they would not have come to that Council. To which we may add, that those *Fathers of Constance* (it will highly concern *Protestant Princes* to *consider it*) Synodically define, and *declare* ; That *all Heretiques*, (that is all they call (and commonly miscall Heretiques) all their *defendors*, or *favourers*, &c. of what *dignity soever*, (*1*) (*Kings*, and *Queens*, and *Dukes*, &c.) shall be Excommunicated and deprived of all their Goods, and Secular Dignities. This (*in Thesi*) is their *impious Doctrine* and *Principle* ; and (*in Praxi*) they are now endeavouring to put it in Execution here in *England* ; as evidently appears by their Popish and Hellish Conspiracy, by the Gracious and Powerful Providence of Heaven, lately and happily discovered. I take it then to be evident, that the aforesaid Popish Doctrines and Principles are exceeding dangerous, and to all Supreme Powers (especially Protestant Kings and Princes) pernicious.

(1) *OMNES & singulos Hæreticos, nec non eorum sectatores utriusque sexus ; & etiam defendentes eosdem, vel ipsis quomodolibet , publice vel occultè participantes ; etiam si REGALI, REGINALI, DUCALI aut alia QUAVIS DIGNITATE Ecclesiasticâ aut mundana præfulgeant ;...... per Excommunicationis,& PRIVATIONIS bonorum ac dignitatum secularium, & alias pœnas etiam per captiones & INCARCERATIONES puniantar.* Concil. Constansienf. Sess. 45.

2 And from the Premises, it will as evidently follow , that the aforesaid Popish Principles, are not the private opinions of some particular persons onely : seeing, 1. They are profess'd and vindicated by the Jesuites, Canonists, and generally by other *great-Writers* of that *Church*, in their Books publish'd with the *approbation* and *commendation* of *Authority*. 2. *Establish'd*
in

in their approved and *received Canon-Law*.
3. In the *Authentick Decretal* Epistles, and *Papal Constitutions*. 4. In their *General Councils*; those (I mean) which they acknowledge to be General. 5. And (to say no more) all their Clergy and Ecclesiastiques, (who have place in *those Councils*) have taken a *Solemn Oath* to maintain *all those Canons*, and *Papal Constitutions*; and this Oath required and taken by the Authority and Command of the (*a*) *Council of Trent*, and the (*b*) *Pope*; who is acknowledged to be their (*c*) Supreme Judge, and (since the Councils of *Pisa*, *Constance* and *Basil*, declared by Pope *Leo the Tenth*, and his *Lateral Council*, (which they account a General Council) to be above all *General Councils*: and this Declaration (that all might know it is Law and Obligatory) has lately been (*d*) referr'd into the *Body of their Canon-Law*. Now these things being undeniably true, that their Popes and General Councils (the Supreme Authority of their Church) have approved and received the aforesaid Principles and Positions, and caused their Ecclesiastiques solemnly to swear, That they do believe, and will constantly profess them, and (so far as they are able) make all committed to their charge, do so too: it evidently follows, that they are *Roman-Catholick Doctrines*, own'd and approved by *their Church*, and not only by private and particular persons. So that if any (who knows, and has impartially consider'd the Premises) deny it;

(*a*) Vide Concil. Trident. Sess. 24. Cap. 12. de Reformat. & Annotat. Joh. Sotellii Theolog. & Doratii Latii, juriconsult., ad caput dictum in 1 S. edit. Concilii Ad.v.p. 15 6. et seque superius.
(*b*) In Bulla Pii Papæ 4. super forma Juramenti professionis Fidei, Romæ 1165.
(*c*) Concil. Florent. Decreto 4. apud Longum a Coriolano, p. g. 836.

(*d*) Cap. *Pastor* 1, Extra *De Conciliis*, in Septimo. And in the same place, Cap *Sicut*, &c. and Cap. *Benedictus* 14. The same Doctrine is confirmed by Pope *Pius* 4.

it; I shall not call him Impudent, but I may (and must) say, he has a hard Forehead, and a little thing will not make him blush.

To conclude; If that Priest, or Popish Gentleman, (you mention) who so confidently denies the Church of *Rome* to approve such Principles, as I have laid to her charge; can either shew,

1. That I have *misquoted* the Authors and Books I cite, and that such Passages do not occur in the places quoted.

2. Or (if they do occur) that I have *mistook* their meaning.

3. Or (if neither of these can be shown) if he can make it appear, that the Church of *Rome* has (by any publick Act or Declaration) disown'd such pernicious Principles and Positions, and damn'd them as erroneous, and (what they really are) impious: I do hereby promise him, that I will be (what I hope I never shall be) one of the worst sort of Christians in the World, I mean a Roman-Catholique. Farewel.

Your Faithful Friend,

T. L.

www.ingramcontent.com/pod-product-compliance
Lightning Source LLC
Chambersburg PA
CBHW022143160426
43197CB00009B/1409